CHAIM WEIZMANN

CHAIM WEIZMANN

Richard Amdur

CHELSEA HOUSE PUBLISHERS

NEW YORK

NEW HAVEN   PHILADELPHIA

Chelsea House Publishers
EDITOR-IN-CHIEF: Nancy Toff
EXECUTIVE EDITOR: Remmel T. Nunn
MANAGING EDITOR: Karyn Gullen Browne
COPY CHIEF: Juliann Barbato
PICTURE EDITOR: Adrian G. Allen
ART DIRECTOR: Giannella Garrett
MANUFACTURING MANAGER: Gerald Levine

World Leaders—Past & Present
SENIOR EDITOR: John W. Selfridge

Staff for CHAIM WEIZMANN:
ASSISTANT EDITOR: Maria Behan
COPY EDITOR: Terrance Dolan
DEPUTY COPY CHIEF: Ellen Scordato
EDITORIAL ASSISTANT: Marie Claire Cebrián
PICTURE RESEARCHER: Emily Miller
DESIGNER: David Murray
PRODUCTION COORDINATOR: Joseph Romano
COVER ILLUSTRATION: Kye Carbone

First Printing

1 3 5 7 9 8 6 4 2

Library of Congress Cataloging in Publication Data

Amdur, Richard.
Chaim Weizmann.

(World leaders past & present)
Bibliography: p.
Includes index.
   Summary: Presents a biography of the leader who worked to establish a
national homeland for Jews in Palestine and served as Israel's first
president in 1949.

1. Weizmann, Chaim, 1874–1952—Juvenile literature.
2. Zionists—Biography—Juvenile literature. 3. Israel—
Presidents—Biography—Juvenile literature. [1. Weizmann,
Chaim, 1874–1952. 2. Zionists. 3. Israel—Presidents]
I. Title. II. Series.
DS125.3.W45A84   1988   956.94′05′0924 [B] [92]   88-5041

ISBN 0-87754-446-8

Contents

John Adams
John Quincy Adams
Konrad Adenauer
Alexander the Great
Salvador Allende
Marc Antony
Corazon Aquino
Yasir Arafat
King Arthur
Hafez al-Assad
Kemal Atatürk
Attila
Clement Attlee
Augustus Caesar
Menachem Begin
David Ben-Gurion
Otto von Bismarck
Léon Blum
Simon Bolívar
Cesare Borgia
Willy Brandt
Leonid Brezhnev
Julius Caesar
John Calvin
Jimmy Carter
Fidel Castro
Catherine the Great
Charlemagne
Chiang Kai-Shek
Winston Churchill
Georges Clemenceau
Cleopatra
Constantine the Great
Hernán Cortés
Oliver Cromwell
Georges-Jacques
   Danton
Jefferson Davis
Moshe Dayan
Charles de Gaulle
Eamon De Valera
Eugene Debs
Deng Xiaoping
Benjamin Disraeli
Alexander Dubček
François & Jean-Claude
   Duvalier
Dwight Eisenhower
Eleanor of Aquitaine
Elizabeth I
Faisal
Ferdinand & Isabella
Francisco Franco
Benjamin Franklin

Frederick the Great
Indira Gandhi
Mohandas Gandhi
Giuseppe Garibaldi
Amin & Bashir Gemayel
Genghis Khan
William Gladstone
Mikhail Gorbachev
Ulysses S. Grant
Ernesto "Che" Guevara
Tenzin Gyatso
Alexander Hamilton
Dag Hammarskjöld
Henry VIII
Henry of Navarre
Paul von Hindenburg
Hirohito
Adolf Hitler
Ho Chi Minh
King Hussein
Ivan the Terrible
Andrew Jackson
James I
Wojciech Jaruzelski
Thomas Jefferson
Joan of Arc
Pope John XXIII
Pope John Paul II
Lyndon Johnson
Benito Juárez
John Kennedy
Robert Kennedy
Jomo Kenyatta
Ayatollah Khomeini
Nikita Khrushchev
Kim Il Sung
Martin Luther King, Jr.
Henry Kissinger
Kublai Khan
Lafayette
Robert E. Lee
Vladimir Lenin
Abraham Lincoln
David Lloyd George
Louis XIV
Martin Luther
Judas Maccabeus
James Madison
Nelson & Winnie
   Mandela
Mao Zedong
Ferdinand Marcos
George Marshall

Mary, Queen of Scots
Tomáš Masaryk
Golda Meir
Klemens von Metternich
James Monroe
Hosni Mubarak
Robert Mugabe
Benito Mussolini
Napoléon Bonaparte
Gamal Abdel Nasser
Jawaharlal Nehru
Nero
Nicholas II
Richard Nixon
Kwame Nkrumah
Daniel Ortega
Mohammed Reza Pahlavi
Thomas Paine
Charles Stewart
   Parnell
Pericles
Juan Perón
Peter the Great
Pol Pot
Muammar el-Qaddafi
Ronald Reagan
Cardinal Richelieu
Maximilien Robespierre
Eleanor Roosevelt
Franklin Roosevelt
Theodore Roosevelt
Anwar Sadat
Haile Selassie
Prince Sihanouk
Jan Smuts
Joseph Stalin
Sukarno
Sun Yat-sen
Tamerlane
Mother Teresa
Margaret Thatcher
Josip Broz Tito
Toussaint L'Ouverture
Leon Trotsky
Pierre Trudeau
Harry Truman
Queen Victoria
Lech Walesa
George Washington
Chaim Weizmann
Woodrow Wilson
Xerxes
Emiliano Zapata
Zhou Enlai

CHELSEA HOUSE PUBLISHERS

ON LEADERSHIP

Arthur M. Schlesinger, jr.

LEADERSHIP, it may be said, is really what makes the world go round. Love no doubt smooths the passage; but love is a private transaction between consenting adults. Leadership is a public transaction with history. The idea of leadership affirms the capacity of individuals to move, inspire, and mobilize masses of people so that they act together in pursuit of an end. Sometimes leadership serves good purposes, sometimes bad; but whether the end is benign or evil, great leaders are those men and women who leave their personal stamp on history.

Now, the very concept of leadership implies the proposition that individuals can make a difference. This proposition has never been universally accepted. From classical times to the present day, eminent thinkers have regarded individuals as no more than the agents and pawns of larger forces, whether the gods and goddesses of the ancient world or, in the modern era, race, class, nation, the dialectic, the will of the people, the spirit of the times, history itself. Against such forces, the individual dwindles into insignificance.

So contends the thesis of historical determinism. Tolstoy's great novel *War and Peace* offers a famous statement of the case. Why, Tolstoy asked, did millions of men in the Napoleonic Wars, denying their human feelings and their common sense, move back and forth across Europe slaughtering their fellows? "The war," Tolstoy answered, "was bound to happen simply because it was bound to happen." All prior history predetermined it. As for leaders, they, Tolstoy said, "are but the labels that serve to give a name to an end and, like labels, they have the least possible connection with the event." The greater the leader, "the more conspicuous the inevitability and the predestination of every act he commits." The leader, said Tolstoy, is "the slave of history."

Determinism takes many forms. Marxism is the determinism of class. Nazism the determinism of race. But the idea of men and women as the slaves of history runs athwart the deepest human instincts. Rigid determinism abolishes the idea of human freedom—

the assumption of free choice that underlies every move we make, every word we speak, every thought we think. It abolishes the idea of human responsibility, since it is manifestly unfair to reward or punish people for actions that are by definition beyond their control. No one can live consistently by any deterministic creed. The Marxist states prove this themselves by their extreme susceptibility to the cult of leadership.

More than that, history refutes the idea that individuals make no difference. In December 1931 a British politician crossing Park Avenue in New York City between 76th and 77th Streets around 10:30 P.M. looked in the wrong direction and was knocked down by an automobile—a moment, he later recalled, of a man aghast, a world aglare: "I do not understand why I was not broken like an eggshell or squashed like a gooseberry." Fourteen months later an American politician, sitting in an open car in Miami, Florida, was fired on by an assassin; the man beside him was hit. Those who believe that individuals make no difference to history might well ponder whether the next two decades would have been the same had Mario Constasino's car killed Winston Churchill in 1931 and Giuseppe Zangara's bullet killed Franklin Roosevelt in 1933. Suppose, in addition, that Adolf Hitler had been killed in the street fighting during the Munich *Putsch* of 1923 and that Lenin had died of typhus during World War I. What would the 20th century be like now?

For better or for worse, individuals do make a difference. "The notion that a people can run itself and its affairs anonymously," wrote the philosopher William James, "is now well known to be the silliest of absurdities. Mankind does nothing save through initiatives on the part of inventors, great or small, and imitation by the rest of us—these are the sole factors in human progress. Individuals of genius show the way, and set the patterns, which common people then adopt and follow."

Leadership, James suggests, means leadership in thought as well as in action. In the long run, leaders in thought may well make the greater difference to the world. But, as Woodrow Wilson once said, "Those only are leaders of men, in the general eye, who lead in action. . . . It is at their hands that new thought gets its translation into the crude language of deeds." Leaders in thought often invent in solitude and obscurity, leaving to later generations the tasks of imitation. Leaders in action—the leaders portrayed in this series—have to be effective in their own time.

And they cannot be effective by themselves. They must act in response to the rhythms of their age. Their genius must be adapted, in a phrase of William James's, "to the receptivities of the moment." Leaders are useless without followers. "There goes the mob," said the French politician hearing a clamor in the streets. "I am their leader. I must follow them." Great leaders turn the inchoate emotions of the mob to purposes of their own. They seize on the opportunities of their time, the hopes, fears, frustrations, crises, potentialities. They succeed when events have prepared the way for them, when the community is awaiting to be aroused, when they can provide the clarifying and organizing ideas. Leadership ignites the circuit between the individual and the mass and thereby alters history.

It may alter history for better or for worse. Leaders have been responsible for the most extravagant follies and most monstrous crimes that have beset suffering humanity. They have also been vital in such gains as humanity has made in individual freedom, religious and racial tolerance, social justice, and respect for human rights.

There is no sure way to tell in advance who is going to lead for good and who for evil. But a glance at the gallery of men and women in *World Leaders—Past and Present* suggests some useful tests.

One test is this: Do leaders lead by force or by persuasion? By command or by consent? Through most of history leadership was exercised by the divine right of authority. The duty of followers was to defer and to obey. "Theirs not to reason why / Theirs but to do and die." On occasion, as with the so-called enlightened despots of the 18th century in Europe, absolutist leadership was animated by humane purposes. More often, absolutism nourished the passion for domination, land, gold, and conquest and resulted in tyranny.

The great revolution of modern times has been the revolution of equality. The idea that all people should be equal in their legal condition has undermined the old structure of authority, hierarchy, and deference. The revolution of equality has had two contrary effects on the nature of leadership. For equality, as Alexis de Tocqueville pointed out in his great study *Democracy in America*, might mean equality in servitude as well as equality in freedom.

"I know of only two methods of establishing equality in the political world," Tocqueville wrote. "Rights must be given to every citizen, or none at all to anyone . . . save one, who is the master of all." There was no middle ground "between the sovereignty of all and the absolute power of one man." In his astonishing prediction of 20th-century totalitarian dictatorship, Tocqueville explained how the revolution of equality could lead to the *"Führerprinzip"* and more terrible absolutism than the world had ever known.

But when rights are given to every citizen and the sovereignty of all is established, the problem of leadership takes a new form, becomes more exacting than ever before. It is easy to issue commands and enforce them by the rope and the stake, the concentration camp and the *gulag.* It is much harder to use argument and achievement to overcome opposition and win consent. The Founding Fathers of the United States understood the difficulty. They believed that history had given them the opportunity to decide, as Alexander Hamilton wrote in the first Federalist Paper, whether men are indeed capable of basing government on "reflection and choice, or whether they are forever destined to depend . . . on accident and force."

Government by reflection and choice called for a new style of leadership and a new quality of followership. It required leaders to be responsive to popular concerns, and it required followers to be active and informed participants in the process. Democracy does not eliminate emotion from politics; sometimes it fosters demagoguery; but it is confident that, as the greatest of democratic leaders put it, you cannot fool all of the people all of the time. It measures leadership by results and retires those who overreach or falter or fail.

It is true that in the long run despots are measured by results too. But they can postpone the day of judgment, sometimes indefinitely, and in the meantime they can do infinite harm. It is also true that democracy is no guarantee of virtue and intelligence in government, for the voice of the people is not necessarily the voice of God. But democracy, by assuring the right of opposition, offers built-in resistance to the evils inherent in absolutism. As the theologian Reinhold Niebuhr summed it up, "Man's capacity for justice makes democracy possible, but man's inclination to injustice makes democracy necessary."

A second test for leadership is the end for which power is sought. When leaders have as their goal the supremacy of a master race or the promotion of totalitarian revolution or the acquisition and exploitation of colonies or the protection of greed and privilege or the preservation of personal power, it is likely that their leadership will do little to advance the cause of humanity. When their goal is the abolition of slavery, the liberation of women, the enlargement of opportunity for the poor and powerless, the extension of equal rights to racial minorities, the defense of the freedoms of expression and opposition, it is likely that their leadership will increase the sum of human liberty and welfare.

Leaders have done great harm to the world. They have also conferred great benefits. You will find both sorts in this series. Even "good" leaders must be regarded with a certain wariness. Leaders are not demigods; they put on their trousers one leg after another just like ordinary mortals. No leader is infallible, and every leader needs to be reminded of this at regular intervals. Irreverence irritates leaders but is their salvation. Unquestioning submission corrupts leaders and demeans followers. Making a cult of a leader is always a mistake. Fortunately hero worship generates its own antidote. "Every hero," said Emerson, "becomes a bore at last."

The signal benefit the great leaders confer is to embolden the rest of us to live according to our own best selves, to be active, insistent, and resolute in affirming our own sense of things. For great leaders attest to the reality of human freedom against the supposed inevitabilities of history. And they attest to the wisdom and power that may lie within the most unlikely of us, which is why Abraham Lincoln remains the supreme example of great leadership. A great leader, said Emerson, exhibits new possibilities to all humanity. "We feed on genius. . . . Great men exist that there may be greater men."

Great leaders, in short, justify themselves by emancipating and empowering their followers. So humanity struggles to master its destiny, remembering with Alexis de Tocqueville: "It is true that around every man a fatal circle is traced beyond which he cannot pass; but within the wide verge of that circle he is powerful and free; as it is with man, so with communities."

1

"To Zion! Let Us Go!"

On November 2, 1917, Baron Lionel Walter Rothschild, the renowned English Zionist, received a communication from British foreign secretary Arthur James Balfour. The letter read:

> I have much pleasure in conveying to you, on behalf of His Majesty's Government, the following declaration of sympathy with Jewish Zionist aspirations which has been submitted to, and approved by, the Cabinet:
>
> His Majesty's Government view with favor the establishment in Palestine of a national home for the Jewish people, and will use their best endeavors to facilitate the achievement of this object, it being clearly understood that nothing shall be done which may prejudice the civil and religious rights of the existing non-Jewish communities in Palestine, or the rights and political status enjoyed by Jews in any other country.

This was a brief statement, to be sure, and a vague one as well. But the Balfour Declaration, as it came to be known, marked a turning point in Jewish history. Suddenly, the world's most powerful government had thrown its full support behind the Zionists — activists seeking to reestablish a Jewish state in the Holy Land from which their ancestors had been expelled nearly 2,000 years before.

Difficult things take a long time, the impossible takes a little longer.
—CHAIM WEIZMANN

The prophet Nehemiah supervises the rebuilding of Solomon's Temple on Mount Zion in Jerusalem around 515 B.C. It was destroyed in A.D. 70 by the Romans, who expelled the Jews from Palestine. With the founding of the Zionist movement almost 2,000 years later, the Jewish people finally returned.

Around 1000 B.C., Saul and David, the first Jewish kings, united the various Hebrew tribes, conquered their neighbors, and created Israel. Under their successor, King Solomon, pictured here, ancient Israel reached the height of its prosperity and power.

History is rife with episodes of Jewish triumph and defeat in Palestine. In the 10th century B.C., King Solomon established Jerusalem as the capital of a Hebrew empire that stretched across ancient Palestine, encompassing today's Israel and parts of Lebanon, Syria, Jordan, Iraq, and Egypt. The city, which boasted a magnificent temple, became the center of Jewish religious worship. Jerusalem was razed by the Babylonians in 586 B.C. as part of their dynastic expansion. Most of the Jews were taken to Babylonia to serve as slaves, an event referred to by the Jews as the Diaspora (a derivation of the Greek word for dispersion). In the 2nd century B.C., a revolt headed by Judah Maccabee led to the reestablishment of a powerful Jewish state in Palestine, but the nation later fell under Roman domination. The Jewish population in Palestine dwindled as time passed. But wherever they lived, Jews remembered the glories and tribulations of their history in the region. Many pledged to return some day to Jerusalem. Over the centuries, Zion, the hill where Solomon's temple once stood, became synonymous with Palestine as the Jewish homeland. Given this history, many Jews in the early 20th century were hopeful that a show of support from a nation as powerful as Great Britain might finally make Zion a reality.

The motives behind the declaration were complex. Apparently the British thought that backing Jewish claims to Palestine would legitimize their presence in the Middle East as World War I drew to a close. The declaration was made as British troops stood poised to capture much of the area from the Turks who ruled Palestine as part of the Ottoman Empire. The war was not yet over, however, and the British government hoped that the declaration would win increased Jewish support for the war effort.

The Roman expulsion orders of A.D. 70 and 135 scattered the Jewish people throughout the world. During the medieval era, the image of the "wandering Jew" embodied the concept of a people deprived of their homeland and living as outcasts in foreign lands.

Chaim Weizmann, the leading spokesman for Zionism throughout the first half of the 20th century, stands at the center of a crowd in his adopted home of Rehovot, Palestine, in 1917, when the British conquered the region from Turkey. Rehovot was one of many Jewish settlements established in Palestine at the start of the century.

Although these considerations make perfect sense, historians agree that England would not have arrived at any of these conclusions on its own. One individual spearheaded efforts to convince Britain to issue the Balfour Declaration. His task was a difficult one, because he represented a scattered people without a nation, a people whose interests conflicted with those of the Arabs — a group of considerable economic and strategic importance to Great Britain. As one historian pointed out, the declaration was "one of the most improbable acts in the history of British foreign policy." It took Chaim Weizmann to make the improbable a reality.

Weizmann, a Russian Jew, had moved to England in 1904 and made a name for himself there as a prominent Zionist spokesman and brilliant scientist. It was in the latter role that the British found Weizmann a most capable ally. In 1915, as World War I raged on, Britain faced a severe munitions shortage. Weizmann's scientific genius enabled him to develop an alternative method for the manufacture of explosives. Reporting directly to Winston Churchill, then first lord of the admiralty, he took on the enormous task of turning his lab research into a large-scale industrial operation of vital importance to the war effort. Weizmann's work "absolutely saved the British army," said David Lloyd George, then minister of munitions. Offered a peerage (a title of nobility) in reward for his feat, Weizmann asked for something else entirely — an official statement of support for his consuming passion, Zionism.

Weizmann began the long and arduous task of winning British backing for the Jews' dream of re-establishing a nation in their ancestral land, Palestine. His contribution to the war effort had earned him access to the British decision-making elite. Lloyd George, who became prime minister, and Winston Churchill, who succeeded him as minister of munitions (and subsequently became secretary for war), had attained positions of real power and could both be said to "owe" Weizmann a favor. Besides drawing on these contacts, he arranged an estimated 2,000 meetings with officials, saw the statement through 5 drafts, and endured a rollercoaster ride of dashed hopes and raised expectations.

Weizmann faced obstacles within the Jewish community, as well. Some Jews felt threatened by Zionism, fearing that their loyalty to England (or any other country in which they lived) would be questioned if they supported the establishment of a Jewish nation in Palestine. Others worried that the growing Zionist movement would antagonize the Turks, who would in turn make life difficult for the Jews already in the Holy Land. And a few thought that Britain would merely pay lip service to the Zionist ideal in order to legitimize its presence in Palestine.

At one point, buffeted by such conflicting sentiments, Weizmann threatened to end his efforts and resign from the presidency of the English Zionist Federation. But he was convinced otherwise by the almost biblical logic of Ahad Ha'am, another prominent Jewish leader, who said: "To whom do you offer your resignation? Who has appointed you? *Fate* has appointed you, and only to *fate* can you offer your resignation."

[The Balfour Declaration was]
the greatest diplomatic coup of
the first world war.
—CHARLES WEBSTER
historian

On October 31, 1917, the British cabinet met to consider the fifth and final draft of the statement on the country's position on a Jewish nation in Palestine. An impatient Weizmann paced outside the conference room like an expectant father. At the session's end one of the ministers emerged and presented Weizmann with a document, saying, "Dr. Weizmann, it's a boy!" Weizmann recalled in his autobiography, "Well — I did not like the boy at first. He was not the one I had expected."

Weizmann had hoped for a more forthright statement, something more explicit. Still, he recognized the importance of the occasion. A crucial first step toward securing a Jewish state had been taken, and he realized he could not expect much more at the moment. After all, this was the great British Empire he was dealing with, and he represented a scattered nation.

Weizmann telephoned his wife, Vera, with the good news and then ran off to tell Ha'am in person. That night, they and friends performed traditional Jewish dances in celebration. The declaration was formally issued on November 2, and Jewish history was changed forever. The Zionist fantasy had, in the space of a single paragraph, entered the real world of politics, the world of the possible.

Early Jewish settlers clearing land in Palestine. Zionist organizations purchased tracts of land from the Turkish administration; as the number of Jewish settlers increased, the native Arab population began to resent what they saw as encroachment on their lands.

The Balfour Declaration led to the creation of the state of Israel — but only after more than 30 years of turmoil, bloodshed, and warfare. Weizmann would remain steadfast throughout this long struggle until he could take his place as president of the newly created nation in 1948. Weizmann was 73 when he realized the dream he had harbored since boyhood. During his youth he had written a letter to one of his teachers professing his hopes for the future of the Jewish people. The letter read, in part: "Let us carry our banner to Zion and return to our first mother upon whose knees we were born. . . . To Zion!—Jews—to Zion! let us go."

The Balfour Declaration represented a midway point in Weizmann's long, often lonely battle to win a Jewish state. But in November 1917, Weizmann did not know what a long road lay ahead. A modest man, he would underplay his achievements; for in obtaining the Balfour Declaration he had placed world Jewry on the map — and had himself become the most important Jewish leader in the world.

Weizmann with British foreign secretary A. J. Balfour (right). In 1917, Balfour issued a statement declaring that the British government supported "the establishment in Palestine of a national home for the Jewish people." The Balfour Declaration was the first step toward the creation of a Jewish state.

2

Escape from the Pale

Chaim Weizmann was born on November 27, 1874, in the small Russian village of Motol. As Weizmann wrote in his memoirs, "Motol was situated in one of the darkest and most forlorn corners of the Pale of Settlement." The Pale, which he termed a "prison-house," was a region along Russia's western frontier, the only place in the country where Jews could legally reside. About 5 million Jews lived there in poverty and under the constant threat of persecution and periodic massacres known as pogroms.

One such series of massacres occurred in 1882, when a Jewish woman was found to be among the conspirators who had assassinated Russia's ruler, Tsar Alexander II, the previous year. Jews as a group were blamed for the national misfortune of Alexander's death. They became scapegoats as unruly mobs released their rage and helplessness through acts of violence. The tsar's murder also prompted a series of regulations known as the May Laws, which further restricted the Jews' legal areas of residence and limited the types of jobs and education they could seek.

All about, in hundreds of towns and villages, Jews lived, as they had lived for many generations, scattered islands in a Gentile ocean.
—CHAIM WEIZMANN
on the Pale of Settlement

Chaim Weizmann as a student in Pinsk, a city in his native Byelorussia, a Russian province. The Byelorussian village in which Weizmann was born in 1874 was located in an impoverished region called the Pale, the only part of Russia that Jews could legally inhabit.

A policeman beating a Jew in 19th-century Russia. The 5 million Jews of tsarist Russia were subjected to frequent riots, called pogroms, in which Christians would descend on Jewish villages to burn and loot homes and shops, beating or killing the Jews themselves. The police and army often participated in pogroms.

As government-sanctioned oppression and anti-Jewish violence flourished in Russia, disturbing trends were also taking place in the supposedly more enlightened corners of Europe. Some Europeans resented the social and economic success that many Jews had achieved. Because religious prejudice was becoming increasingly unacceptable in "modern" Europe, the persecution of Jews took on a new form: Oppression was based on racial, not religious, grounds. Although Jews are united by religious heritage, not race, this new form of bigotry, called anti-Semitism (Semite is the name of the race that includes Jews and Arabs), was common during the late 19th century.

Compared to many other Russian Jews, Chaim's family fared rather well. His parents, Ozer and Rachel Weizmann, were 15 and 14 years old, respectively, when they were married. Chaim was the third of their 15 children, 12 of whom survived into adulthood. Ozer Weizmann supported his large family by selling timber, this being the main occupation in a town set amid large forests. He saw his fortunes fluctuate — his was a seasonal trade greatly dependent on weather conditions — but generally improve over time. The Weizmanns lived in a large house situated on a sizable plot of land where the family grew its own vegetables and raised chickens and cows.

Chaim and his siblings grew up in an atmosphere that combined age-old Jewish traditions with modern sensibilities. Their home was filled with books published in three languages — Yiddish, Hebrew, and Russian. (Yiddish originated with the Jews of central and eastern Europe and was the most common spoken language in the Pale, Hebrew was the formal language of Jewish writings, and Russian was the language of the rest of the nation.) The family bookshelves displayed not only books by great Russian writers such as Maxim Gorky, Leo Tolstoy, and Anton Chekhov but also works by Hebrew thinkers such as Maimonides, a 12th-century scholar and philosopher. Zionist periodicals also made their way into the household. "The return [to Palestine] was in the air," Weizmann later said of Motol, "a hope which would not die."

Two Jews in the ruins of their home after a pogrom in Sochoczow, Poland. For almost 2,000 years, the Jews of Europe had been subjected to repeated massacres, riots, confiscations of property, expulsions, forced ghettoizations, and every other possible form of persecution.

Early in his childhood Chaim showed a natural sense of diplomacy. According to Rachel Weizmann, one day she, her husband, and young Chaim were walking home from a religious service when she happened to look through a neighbor's window and notice silver candlesticks that looked suspiciously like her own. Although she was angry and wanted to reclaim her property immediately, her son counseled patience. Rachel Weizmann reported that Chaim told her, "Today is a great festival, Mother. Do not embarrass those people on a holy day. It would be better if you wait until after the festival has ended." She recognized a certain wisdom in the young boy's words and heeded his advice — but never did get her candlesticks back.

In his youth Chaim's father had studied with a rabbi, yet he was known occasionally to flout Jewish convention in his adult years. For one thing, Ozer Weizmann smoked on the Sabbath, a small act that nevertheless set him apart from his more devout neighbors. And, though Jewish women were expected to serve primarily as homemakers, Ozer Weizmann planned to send not only his sons but also his daughters to school. Finally, in something of an unprecedented step for a family in a village such as Motol, he decided to send Chaim and his older brother 25 miles from home to study in Pinsk, a city that boasted a modern-style school. Weizmann was determined that his sons would learn as much as they could of the world outside the Pale of Settlement.

Two Russian Jewish pharmacists pose in their shop; a photo of the tsar hangs above the clock on the wall behind them. Zionism first evolved in Eastern Europe as a response to the systematic anti-Semitism of the region, asserting that Jews could only be free if they lived in their own state.

Weizmann at the age of 10. The third of 15 children in his family, he showed great interest and talent in literature and science. One year after this picture was taken, he was sent from his small village of Motol to Pinsk, the nearest city, to attend a Jewish secondary school.

Chaim was 11 years old when he was sent to Pinsk, and he later wrote of the city in mixed terms. On the one hand, he described it as a place that was years ahead of his native village: "There was a high school — the one I was going to attend — there were libraries, hospitals, factories, and paved streets." But on another occasion, he characterized Pinsk as "God-forsaken — not a town but an enormous rubbish-heap, with hundreds of Jews pushing and hurrying through the streets, their anxious faces marked by great suffering, and moving as in a daze."

For his first three years in Pinsk, Chaim lodged with friends of the family. Subsequently he moved in with the Luries, a prominent Jewish family with business and banking interests around the Continent. He tutored the Luries' youngest son, Saul, in exchange for room, board, and a small amount of money that paid for his living expenses.

Ozer and Rachel Weizmann, Chaim's parents. Ozer was a lumber merchant in Motol who eventually built up a prosperous business. The family lived in a relatively large home and owned a substantial collection of books that included works in Yiddish, classical Hebrew, and modern Russian.

His association with the Luries served him well. As the rapid technological expansion known as the Industrial Revolution began to be felt in Russia, the Luries opened a chemical works. Chaim, already interested in a career in chemistry, spent long hours at the plant, experimenting and refining his skills.

He learned more about chemistry through his personal reading and observations at the Luries' factory than he did at school. Although the education he received in Pinsk was certainly more far-reaching than any he could have had in his native village, his school was still bound by religious conventions. Only rarely did his teachers go beyond the rigid curriculum prescribed by Jewish tradition. Once, one of his teachers allowed the students to read aloud from a Hebrew chemistry book — but only in a way that would not arouse suspicion. "We read," wrote Weizmann, "in the Talmudic chant hallowed by tradition, so that anyone passing by the school would never suspect that we were not engaged in the sacred pursuits proper to a Hebrew school."

Pinsk was the center for an early Zionist group called the Hovevei Zion (Lovers of Zion), and Chaim was eventually drawn into the movement. The movement's leader was Leo Pinsker, who described the group's guiding principles in an 1882 pamphlet called *Auto-Emancipation*. Pinsker maintained that anti-Semitism was a disease that Gentiles (non-Jews) could not seem to overcome. Jews could escape persecution, he believed, only by forsaking gentile society and gathering together in a country of their own. As Chaim became increasingly involved with the Hovevei Zion, he heard a great deal about Jewish pioneers—brave men and women who were leaving Europe in increasing numbers to settle in Palestine in the hopes of establishing a homeland there. By 1890 he thought of himself as a committed Zionist.

Weizmann graduated from his secondary school as a star pupil and was determined to continue his education. Thus, he faced a difficult choice regarding his future. He could stay in Russia, near his family, and struggle through a segregated school system seemingly designed to squelch Jewish ambition. Or he could journey westward to one of the famous European learning centers, where he would face the trauma of being far from home and family. Finally, Weizmann made his choice: "I disliked Russia intensely, not Russia proper, that is, but tsarist Russia. All my inclinations pointed to the West, whither thousands of Russian Jewish students had moved by now, in a sort of educational stampede."

A friend helped him obtain a job as a Hebrew and Russian teacher at a Jewish boarding school in Pfungstadt, Germany. The Darmstadt Polytechnic, where he could take college-preparation courses in chemistry, was less than an hour away by train. The only thing that stood in his way was a lack of the funds necessary to obtain a passport.

Young Chaim Weizmann cleverly found another way out of the country. "I became," he later wrote, "a raft worker, and as such entitled to make the round trip on the river to Danzig without a foreign passport. At Thorn, the first stop on German territory, I picked up my bundles and skipped. It was a marvelous new world that I entered."

3

Coming of Age in the West

The enthusiasm 19-year-old Chaim Weizmann felt as he first set foot on German soil wore off all too quickly. Financial necessity and ambition soon drove him to undertake an exhausting routine of work and study. Yet the daily grind of attending classes at Darmstadt Polytechnic and teaching his pupils at the Jewish boarding school paled beside a problem that he had never encountered before — one that cut to the core of the young Zionist's beliefs.

Weizmann was disappointed in the Jews of Germany. Most of them, he found, had adapted to German culture so wholeheartedly that their distinct identity as Jews had become virtually nonexistent. Threatened by prejudice, many German Jews wanted to be perceived as Germans, not Jews. Weizmann found this tendency unsettling — and dangerous. As he put it, Jews who felt they had eluded persecution by blending in with the larger population were in "the high summer of their illusory security." Perhaps because anti-Semitism was so blatant in his native land, he did not believe that Jews could escape from age-old prejudices simply by adopting the ways of another culture.

Anti-Semitism was an open fact of daily life in Russia, practised as government policy. Here, in the focus of Europe, it was a subtle human reflex.
—BARNET LITVINOFF
on anti-Jewish prejudice in Germany

Berlin at the turn of the century. Germany, then perhaps the world's wealthiest nation, was home to a large and prosperous Jewish population. When Weizmann arrived there, he was struck by how fully the country's Jews had shed their Jewish identity and become assimilated into German culture.

Discrimination against Jews was less severe in much of Western and Central Europe, leading many Jews to abandon traditional customs and seek advancement through assimilation. But in Eastern Europe, where discrimination was harsh, Jews such as these in Dubrovnik tended to retain traditional ways.

On a much deeper level, he was hurt that many of Germany's Jews seemed to consider German culture superior to their own. As Weizmann later remarked: "In Russia at least we, the Jews, had a culture of our own, and a high one. We had standing in our own eyes. We did not dream that our Jewish being was something to be sloughed off furtively." He continued: "But in Germany, surrounded by efficiency and power, the Jews were obsessed by a sense of inferiority which urged them ceaselessly to deny themselves and to regard their heritage with shame — and at the same time to sing their own praises in the ears of those who would not listen."

Weizmann's time as a student in Germany was not a happy one. In a typical day he rose at 5:00 A.M., arrived via train in Darmstadt at 6:30, and then walked the streets for an hour until the university opened. After a full day of classes — in German, which Weizmann spoke at a level well beneath that of his professors and fellow students — he would arrive back in Pfungstadt by 4:00 P.M., teach Russian and Hebrew until 6:00, and then work late into the night on his homework and on his German. His daytime meal consisted of bread, sausage, and cheese, in meager portions, and dinner, he said in his memoirs, was a similarly "wretched affair."

Weizmann ended his studies in Darmstadt after two dispiriting semesters. Then, after a year at home, he set out for the more encouraging atmosphere of Germany's capital, Berlin, where he had been accepted by the chemistry school of the prestigious Charlottenberg Technical College. Berlin proved to be a turning point for Weizmann in almost all regards. "In Berlin I grew out of my boyhood Zionism," he later recalled, "out of my adolescence, into something like maturity. When I left Berlin . . . the adult pattern of my life was set."

It was in Berlin that Weizmann began to live the dual life he would lead for the rest of his years — a life that blended a love of science with a passion for Zionism. In the scientific realm, he was able to study and find employment in an environment that was on the cutting edge of the industrial boom occurring throughout the country and much of the world. As for his Zionism, Weizmann quickly fell in with a group of intellectuals from the Russo-Jewish Academic Society, an organization that he later said could be considered the "cradle of the modern Zionist movement."

One of the society's members was Asher Ginsberg, better known as Ahad Ha'am, a Hebrew name that translates as "one of the people." Ha'am, a Russian Jew born in 1856, did not think it possible, or desirable, for the masses of European Jews to settle in the Holy Land. Rather, he said, Palestine should be a spiritual or cultural center for world Judaism, an example and cohesive force for world Jewry,

Ahad Ha'am, an early Zionist theoretician, stressed the importance of reaching an agreement with the Arabs of Palestine. Ha'am advocated a slow settlement process: "Develop Hebrew culture in the Diaspora first," he wrote, "so as to make the people worthy of nationhood." Weizmann was deeply influenced by Ha'am.

For centuries, Palestinian Arabs had lived in Palestine, the region designated by Zionists for the settlement of Jews. Though some Palestinian Arabs were Christian, the vast majority were Muslim. The Apostles' Spring, a site sacred to Christianity, is pictured here.

which he feared was in a state of disintegration. "Don't rush things in Palestine," he wrote in one of his many essays, "or we shall create little of permanent value there."

Ha'am was also among the first thinkers to point out that Zionists would have to reach a humane settlement with the Arabs who had been living in Palestine for many centuries. This idea was controversial, for in some respects it implied a reining in of the Zionist vision. But although many Jews rejected the particulars of Ha'am's message, his depth of thought and sound moral foundation attracted many followers. Among them was Chaim Weizmann, who shared Ha'am's belief that Zionism should never sacrifice humane principles in the interests of political expediency. Weizmann also adopted Ha'am's patient approach, a fact that would alienate some of his fellow Zionists in later years. As historian and Weizmann biographer Norman Rose pointed out, Weizmann "strived all his life to attain a working synthesis between the spiritualism of Ahad Ha'am and his stratagems as leader of a political movement."

The debates about Zionism were not limited to the Jews of Berlin. As the 19th century drew to a close, unrest was growing in Jewish communities across Europe. As Weizmann put it, there was a "vague, groping, unformulated" impulse for "Jewish self-determination." The feeling arose for many reasons, perhaps foremost among them a simple realization: that the Jews, despite many years of contribution to European society and presumed assimilation into its ranks, had failed to gain true acceptance.

In 1896 a Hungarian-born journalist named Theodor Herzl published *Der Judenstaat* (The Jewish State). Herzl, who had recently been a Paris correspondent for a Vienna, Austria, newspaper, had been prompted to write his book by his experiences of anti-Semitism in these European capitals. The most shocking of these was the Dreyfus affair.

In 1894 the French government accused a Jewish army officer named Alfred Dreyfus of passing important military information on to the Germans. He was convicted of treason and condemned to life imprisonment. Herzl covered the Dreyfus trial for his newspaper and witnessed mobs shouting "Death to the Jews" during the court proceedings. Despite evidence that Dreyfus was innocent, it was not until 1906 that the government acknowledged the conviction's anti-Semitic roots and overturned it as "wrongful" and "erroneous."

By then the damage had been done — the depth of anti-Semitism in France had been exposed. Jews the world over were stunned, because most of them had considered France one of the most enlightened and liberal countries in Europe. Like many others, Herzl reasoned that if such a thing could happen in France, Jews were not safe anywhere. In *Der Judenstaat*, he argued that Jews could live in freedom and with dignity only if they had a land of their own.

The response to Herzl's book was passionate, and much of it was negative. Religious Jews, especially rabbis, opposed Herzl on theological grounds — they believed that the Jewish state would be resurrected only with the coming of the Hebrew savior and that it was sacrilege for men to try to do the work of God.

Theodore Herzl, here wearing a top hat as he leaves a synagogue in Basle, Switzerland, in 1903, was recognized as the father of modern Zionism. A lawyer and journalist, in 1896 he wrote *The Jewish State* and laid out the procedure for Zionist settlement of Palestine.

Jews from Eastern Europe were much more receptive to Herzl's ideas than those from the West, a reaction that reflected the different conditions under which they lived. Eastern Europeans lived with the immediacy of pogroms and laws that restricted their lives and livelihoods; Western Europeans were for the most part assimilated Jews who faced more subtle forms of prejudice.

At first, Herzl was often in the frustrating position of preaching to the converted — those who already supported the idea of a Jewish nation — but that would soon change. Herzl's ideas were not new, but his stirring rhetoric captured the imagination, and he soon emerged as Zionism's leading spokesman. In Weizmann's words, "What had emerged from the *Judenstaat* was less a concept than a historic personality."

Der Judenstaat was Herzl's plan for action. The year after its publication, in 1897, he convened the First Zionist Congress, which took place in Basle, Switzerland. The congress established the World Zionist Organization to "create for the Jewish people a home in Palestine secured by public law." Most of the Hovevei Zion chapters joined the World Zionist Organization, which became the largest, and most influential, Zionist group.

In a case that divided France and drew worldwide attention, Captain Alfred Dreyfus, a Jewish officer in the French army, was convicted on trumped-up treason charges in 1894. The case exposed the depth of anti-Semitism in France and gave Zionism a new sense of urgency. Dreyfus was fully exonerated in 1906.

Weizmann, who had returned to Russia to try to sell his discovery of a new process for creating textile dye, did not attend the historic gathering — but it was the only Zionist congress he would ever miss. He served as a delegate to the Second Zionist Congress, held in 1898, also in Basle. He was elected to the Congress Steering Committee, which had a hand in financial matters. Although this was not Weizmann's strong suit, he was happy to be making formal progress within the movement. By this time, he was living in Switzerland, studying at the University at Fribourg in order to complete his doctoral thesis.

In 1900, Herzl convened the congress in London, hoping to expand the Zionist movement in Great Britain, the most powerful nation in Europe. The Third Zionist Congress was important on two counts: The group founded the Jewish National Fund, which became one of the major institutions concerned with purchasing and developing land in Palestine; and Weizmann began to show considerable impatience with Herzl's efforts, voicing the first strains of opposition to the movement's founder.

Herzl had focused much of his energy on obtaining a supportive "charter" from Turkish sultan Abdülhamid II, who ruled Palestine as part of the Ottoman Empire. But Herzl failed to make any headway with the sultan, and was only able to garner halfhearted support for the Zionist cause from such great powers as France and England. Thus, Weizmann thought, Herzl's diplomatic efforts had really

Herzl founded the World Zionist Congress in 1897 and spent the next several years meeting with influential figures to gain support for the organization; in this picture he is bound for Germany and a meeting with Kaiser Wilhelm. Weizmann was elected to the group's financial committee in 1898.

The cover of a special edition of *The World*, a prominent Zionist weekly, reports on a meeting between Herzl and Sultan Abdül Hamid II, ruler of the Ottoman Empire, to discuss Zionist settlement in Palestine. The Ottoman Turks ruled Palestine from 1516 until 1917.

gotten the movement nowhere. Weizmann said that it was the "practical" activists — for example, those willing to move to Palestine and work at establishing new settlements — who would make the difference for Zionism.

He soon found that his feelings were shared by others. During the winter of 1900–1901, Weizmann formed the first opposition group in the Zionist movement — an organization that came to be known as the Democratic Fraction. The group influenced Zionist affairs, especially at the 1902 congress, and helped to frame the general terms of the Zionist debate for some time to come. The organization also served as the vehicle through which Weizmann engineered his rise within Zionist ranks.

Weizmann's achievements in the movement to secure a Jewish state were matched by his successes in the field of chemistry. In 1901 he became a lecturer at Geneva University. That same year he sold his first patent to I. G. Farben, the German industrial giant. Ironically, Farben later played a significant role in fueling the Nazi campaign against the Jews. Weizmann later wrote that "it gives me a queer feeling to remember that I, too, like many another innocent foreign chemist, contributed. . . . to the power of that sinister instrument of German ambition."

In 1903 the Zionist movement was jolted by news that, following the imposition of even more severe strictures on Jewish life in the Pale, a terrible pogrom had been carried out in the Russian town of Kishinev. Forty-nine Jews were killed, hundreds more were injured, shops were looted, and property was destroyed. The Kishinev pogrom served as a painful reminder that the Zionists were, truth be told, no closer to their goal of a homeland than they

Herzl (center) at the first World Zionist Congress in Basle in 1897. Within five years, it became apparent that Herzl's policy of obtaining support from heads of state was failing. He died in 1904 without seeing his dream of a Jewish return to Zion come to pass.

In 1903, a pogrom in Kishinev, Russia, left 49 Jews dead and hundreds more injured, including those pictured here. The violence of the anti-Semitic riot radicalized Zionist opinion and led Weizmann to criticize Herzl's slow approach to implementing Jewish settlement in Palestine.

had been at the First Zionist Congress. The movement's leaders realized that they had spent more time on impassioned internal debates than they had on improving the lives of the world's Jews. On the eve of the Sixth Zionist Congress, held in 1903, Weizmann remarked that the general situation was simply "awful." It was about to get worse.

Speaking to the Zionists assembled for the congress, Theodor Herzl announced that Britain had offered to create a homeland for the Jews. There was one significant drawback, however: The land they were proposing for the project was in East Africa. With Kishinev on his mind, Herzl was interested in an immediate solution to the problems of Jews in Europe, and the British plan offered some hope of reaching that goal. Bitter controversy erupted at the conference: Some agreed with Herzl; others opposed the plan as a perversion of the Zionist dream, ridiculing it as Zionism without Zion.

Indeed, one delegate felt so outraged that she tore down the map of East Africa that had replaced the map of Palestine that usually hung behind the speaker's platform during congress proceedings. Herzl finally gained the support necessary to pursue the plan by stressing that Africa would provide a temporary shelter for the Jews, because Palestine remained central to Zionist hopes.

Weizmann, ever the diplomat and ever the compromiser, was torn. After all, he reasoned, even if the plan was not to everyone's liking, the fact remained that Great Britain was engaging the Zionists in a serious discussion of their fate. Such an offer was not to be taken lightly, nor should the idea be thrown back in its sponsor's face without a fair hearing. But Weizmann remained skeptical. "The conception was at once crude, naive, and generous," he wrote. "There is no immediate solution of great historic problems. There is only movement in the direction of the solution."

The East Africa idea would soon lose what little momentum it had, and Weizmann turned his attention to other matters. The controversy had shown him that Zionism's fate might be tied to Great Britain, so he went to London to assess the general Zionist situation there and to drum up support for a plan he had recently conceived for a university to be built in Palestine. But events proved disappointing: The Democratic Fraction suffered from a lack of zeal, he was unable to get his university plan off the ground, and he failed to win a teaching post he had sought in Palestine. Weizmann returned to Geneva in despair.

Feeling that he had reached something of a dead end and wanting to make a fresh start somewhere, he accepted an offer to teach at Victoria University in Manchester, England. In early July 1904, he was set to leave Switzerland when the news arrived that Herzl — by then a broken, frustrated, and sick man — had died. The Zionists were left in a state of shock, with no heir apparent. After attending a mournful Zionist gathering at the Geneva railway station, Chaim Weizmann, Herzl's as yet unrecognized heir, set off for Great Britain.

We are a people—one people. We are strong enough to form a state and indeed a model state.
—THEODOR HERZL
from *Der Judenstaat*

4

The Great Adventure

When Weizmann arrived in Manchester, England, in 1904, he wanted nothing more than to stay out of Zionist politics, at least for a while. The fractious East Africa debate had taken a toll on his energies. The mourning of Herzl's death had done the same to his emotions. Weizmann, intent on a self-imposed exile in which thought, study, and research were to be his primary activities, had come to the right place.

Manchester is an industrial center located nearly 200 miles northwest of London, Britain's capital. Though this distance is not great, in the scheme of British political and cultural life Manchester in the early 20th century was a backwater. For a scientist such as Weizmann, however, the city's chemical industry and university afforded fertile ground for work. "I lived . . . almost incommunicado," he wrote. "I used to bring my lunch to the lab and work solidly from nine o'clock in the morning till seven or eight at night, or even later; and I continued to fill in my time with the reading of chemical textbooks and articles in chemical reviews."

Vera Chatzman and Chaim Weizmann were married in 1906, six years after they met while both were university students in Geneva. The daughter of a Jewish officer in the Russian army, she grew up knowing little of Judaism, but became an ardent Zionist after meeting her future husband.

A. J. Balfour, then Britain's prime minister, first met Weizmann in 1905 in Manchester, England, where the Zionist leader had moved one year before to work as a chemical researcher. Their meeting established a working relationship that would eventually result in the Balfour Declaration of 1917.

Weizmann's sense of isolation was heightened by his separation from his fiancée, Vera Chatzman, who had remained in Switzerland to finish her medical schooling. The two had met at the Jewish Club in Geneva in 1900. Chatzman, a student at Geneva University, had noticed Weizmann enter the club and engage another student in conversation. She described her initial impression of him in her memoirs, *The Impossible Takes Longer*: "He was pale, dedicated, very frail yet severe, with a faintly ironic gleam in his eyes, mingled with deep and affecting sadness, and he seemed to carry all the burdens of the Jewish world."

These last few words, and Chatzman's presence at the Jewish Club, would seem to indicate that she and Weizmann shared an impassioned commitment to Zionist ideals. In fact, the two were very different, especially in terms of their Jewish identity. Because of his distinguished military service,

Chatzman's father had been accorded special privileges, and the family had been allowed to settle in Rostov-on-Don, a town well outside the Pale of Settlement. Having grown up among Christian Russians, Vera Chatzman learned no Yiddish or Hebrew and very little about Zionism or even Jewish tradition. Yet despite their differences, Weizmann fell deeply in love with her. He was pleased that during the next several years she, too, became an ardent convert to the Zionist cause.

Chatzman visited Manchester once in 1904 and again in 1905. By this time Weizmann had worked his way out of a painful and embarrassing personal dilemma. When he and Vera Chatzman began their romance, he was already engaged to another woman, Sophia Getsova, a dedicated Zionist who was a member of the Democratic Fraction. Friends and family considered the Getsova-Weizmann match ideal, but Weizmann was captivated by Vera Chatzman. It took him two years to disengage himself from this romantic tangle. The stress of breaking things off with his first fiancée was so great that it brought on an outbreak of the painful eye trouble that would recur throughout his life.

The Polish delegation to the Eighth Zionist Congress, held at The Hague, Netherlands, in 1907. At the congress, Weizmann formulated the policy of "practical" Zionism, stating that the Jews who had already settled in Palestine formed the political base for the establishment of a Jewish homeland.

Baron Edmond de Rothschild, from the French branch of the famous Jewish banking family, contributed huge sums to the Zionist effort. In 1913, he donated funds for the establishment of Weizmann's scientific research institute in Jerusalem; it eventually evolved into Hebrew University.

Weizmann and Vera Chatzman were finally married in August 1906. After a "working honeymoon" in Cologne, Germany, where the groom attended Zionist planning sessions, the couple moved into new quarters in Manchester. Their first son, Benjamin, was born in 1907; another child, Michael, followed in 1916. Chaim and Vera Weizmann's marriage would be marked by many work-related separations—and a love that bridged these gaps.

For Weizmann, England meant freedom—as a scientist and also as a Jew. He was living in Manchester, a thriving industrial center that was also a center for chemical research. He was also far from the Pale—and thus removed from the threat of physical harm or displacement. Jews were accepted by much of English society. This was, Weizmann knew, the country in which a Jew, Benjamin Disraeli, had become prime minister and had been a vital voice in the country's affairs during the late 19th century.

Inevitably, Weizmann began to emerge from his academic and scientific cocoon and make contact with English Zionists. Manchester proved to be home to a large number of articulate and influential Jews. Among them were Charles Dreyfus, the owner of a local dyestuffs plant where Weizmann worked as a chemist in the summer of 1905, and Harry Sacher, a reporter for the *Manchester Guardian*. London, meanwhile, had become home to Ahad Ha'am, and Weizmann visited him there regularly.

In 1905, Weizmann, still a newcomer to England, had the good fortune to meet the British prime minister, Arthur James Balfour. Balfour had come to Manchester as part of an election campaign. Remembering the prime minister's desire to discuss Zionism with a leader who opposed the East African plan, his aides arranged a meeting with Weizmann. That encounter has become somewhat legendary in Zionist history, mainly for the forthrightness with which Weizmann addressed England's paramount political figure.

Vladimir Jabotinsky, a Russian Jew and militant Zionist, opposed Weizmann's plan to build a scientific institute in Jerusalem, maintaining instead that a school to educate young Jewish students was more important. During World War I, Jabotinsky, like many Zionists, fought for the British.

According to one account of the meeting, Weizmann asked Balfour, "Supposing I were to offer you Paris instead of London, would you take it?"

"But Dr. Weizmann," replied Balfour, "we have London."

"That is true," said Weizmann. "But we had Jerusalem when London was a marsh."

After a pause, Balfour reportedly asked, "Are there many Jews who think like you?"

"I believe," Weizmann responded, "I speak the mind of millions of Jews whom you will never see and who cannot speak for themselves, but with whom I could pave the streets of the country I come from."

Balfour then said, "If that is so, you will one day be a force."

At the Eighth Zionist Congress, held in the Netherlands in 1907, Weizmann took another big step toward assuming Herzl's mantle. David Wolffsohn, a German Jew and close follower of Herzl, had been elected president at the 1905 congress, but in the view of Weizmann and many others, Wolffsohn was an interim president, a caretaker who would give way once a stronger leader emerged. Weizmann, convinced that he was that man, campaigned hard to remove Wolffsohn from power — and to draw attention to his own ideas.

Weizmann delivered a rousing speech to the congress on what he termed "synthetic Zionism." In his formulation, the achievements of the "practical" settlers in the Yishuv (the Jewish community in Palestine) would create the strongest possible political base for a homeland. The political and practical aspects of realizing the Zionist dream were dependent on one another, Weizmann reasoned: Therefore Zionist leaders must strive for a synthesis between the two concerns. Because Herzl and his followers had relied heavily on the diplomacy and vague agreements favored by the "politicals," Weizmann's speech served as a rallying cry for the Zionists known as the "practicals."

Weizmann made his first visit to Palestine shortly after the 1907 congress. He arrived to find a land that both heartened and saddened him. He wrote

his wife: "It's worth a lifetime to glimpse the work of Jewish hands, to see how after 20 years of toil, former sand and swamp support flourishing orchards, to see Jewish farmers. I understood many things much better, more clearly: the potentiality of Palestine is immense." But Weizmann's enthusiasm about the future of Jewish settlements in the region was tempered by an awareness of the harsh realities of the present. He wrote in his memoirs that the Holy Land was "one of the most neglected corners of the miserably neglected Turkish Empire."

Indeed, Weizmann was not exaggerating: The Yishuv faced an uphill battle. For one thing, the Jews were outnumbered by nearly 10 to 1 in Palestine, a land they were calling their own. Of a total population of some 600,000, Jews numbered about 60,000, with the Muslim community numbering about half a million and Christians making up the rest. Although the Ottoman leaders were eager to sell land to Jewish immigrants in order to bolster their crumbling empire, many Turks were wary of

Jerusalem just prior to the outbreak of World War I in 1914. Of the 600,000 inhabitants of Ottoman-ruled Palestine, 60,000 were Jews. At center is the Dome of the Rock, one of Islam's most sacred sites; the shrine, marking the spot where Mohammed ascended to heaven, is built atop the ruins of the Jews' Second Temple.

the new arrivals because most Jews in Palestine were involved in business or commerce with foreign powers that could, the Turks feared, interfere in the administration of their empire. The local Arab population, too, was alarmed by the prospect of Jewish statehood. They felt that the Jews would rob them of their livelihoods and banish them from their land. Furthermore, many of the Jewish settlements were poorly run, and because they were not self-sufficient, they needed to be kept afloat by money from abroad.

Weizmann returned to England determined to step up his campaign for increased "practical" work in Palestine. In 1913 he revived his plan to build a Jewish university in Jerusalem. He lobbied for the idea at that year's Zionist congress and also managed to enlist the aid of Baron Edmond de Rothschild. Like Lionel Walter Rothschild, his relative in the British branch of the family, French financier Edmond de Rothschild had a passionate interest in Zionism. Gradually, Weizmann gained support for the movement. But in order to win funding from the baron, he had to settle for a compromised version of his original plan. Rothschild, thinking that the establishment of a full-fledged university in Palestine would be somewhat premature, was willing to finance only a research institute. Weizmann accepted the baron's terms, hoping that a university would eventually grow out of the institute.

Some Zionists opposed Weizmann's plan, notably Vladimir Jabotinsky, a militant Russian Jew who later founded the hard-line Revisionist party. Jabotinsky distrusted Rothschild. He said that Palestine needed a university to educate young students, not a research institution "where scientists could work and strive to gain the Nobel prize." Other Zionists maintained that priority should be given to land purchases and economic development before the project was undertaken. Weizmann, a talented speaker, faced down his opposition and won approval for his plan. A site was chosen in Jerusalem — a dramatic perch atop Mount Scopus, a hill near the Mount of Olives, offering a close-up view of the Old City and, in the distance, the Dead Sea

The Austrian archduke Franz Ferdinand and his wife were assassinated in Sarajevo, Bosnia, in June 1914, touching off World War I. The fighting, which involved almost every nation in Europe as well as Ottoman Turkey, delayed Zionist initiatives.

and Judean hills. A final meeting on the project was scheduled for August 12, 1914.

Global events prevented this meeting from occurring. The June assassination of Austrian archduke Franz Ferdinand sparked a rise in international tensions that quickly escalated into World War I. Austria-Hungary, Russia, Germany, France, Great Britain, Turkey, and the United States would eventually join the conflict. When the Turks entered the fray, it looked as if the war would determine the fate of Palestine. The conflict also diverted international attention from the Zionist cause and broke down consensus within the movement. As Weizmann biographer Barnet Litvinoff put it, "With its first shell-burst the war put an end to the old Zionist movement as Theodor Herzl had constituted it. That machine depended upon coordinating the will of men who were primarily Jews. Now they were primarily Englishmen, Russians, Germans, Americans, and they would be swayed not as a single people, but as citizens divided by countries seeking to conquer each other, or to cherish their safety in neutrality."

Although Weizmann wryly noted that "to conduct international Zionist politics during the First World War was to walk on eggs," he faced the difficulties with a new ally. In September 1914 he met C. P. Scott, the owner and editor of the *Manchester Guardian*. Weizmann's eloquence won him an influential supporter, and the two struck an immediate rapport. As a former Liberal member of Parliament, Scott had virtually unlimited access to the leading figures in Great Britain's government. That access soon became Weizmann's, as well.

The *Guardian* became pro-Zionist in tone, and, more important, Scott advocated the Zionist cause to Lloyd George, the minister of munitions who would soon be propelled into the prime ministership. After their first meeting, Lloyd George was so impressed with Weizmann that he wrote to Herbert Samuel, president of the local government board, "When you and I are forgotten, this man will have a monument to him in Palestine."

Turkish and German officers before the Dome of the Rock in Jerusalem. Turkey, Germany, and Austria-Hungary — known as the Central Powers — fought against France, Britain, and Russia. Though Jews served on both sides of the conflict, Zionists fought for Britain because of its sympathies for the movement.

Herbert Samuel, Zionist and member of the British cabinet during World War I. Known as the first practicing Jew to hold a high place in the British government, he, Weizmann, and others successfully lobbied Prime Minister David Lloyd George for British help in establishing a Jewish homeland.

Weizmann's lobbying efforts took on added vigor after these initial forays into Great Britain's corridors of power. He continued to cultivate the Rothschilds of France, renewed his friendship with Balfour, and met an impressive roster of figures from the British decision-making elite. He used these contacts to lay the groundwork for his later efforts, hoping that someday soon, British and Zionist interests would coincide.

In 1915 the British government war office asked the country's scientists to inform the government about any discoveries that might contribute to the war effort. In particular, what the British lacked was acetone, a key ingredient in the manufacture of explosives. Weizmann responded to the call. Working in his Manchester laboratory, he created a process by which acetone could be synthesized through the fermentation of corn mash. When the war office learned of his discovery, he was called down to London and installed as head of the Admiralty Laboratories.

The Weizmanns spent the war years in England, where Chaim's work as a chemical researcher proved vital to the British war effort. He developed a process for making synthetic acetone, a key element used in explosives. He then directed its large-scale manufacture, alleviating a severe ammunition shortage.

Weizmann undertook the enormous task of transforming his research laboratory into a massive industrial operation, and factories using his process to produce acetone sprung up throughout England, relieving the British arms shortage. In time he saw the process used in distilleries in India (then a British colony), France, Canada, and the United States.

Fortunately for the Zionist movement, Weizmann's work for the war effort did not go unrecognized. As Prime Minister Lloyd George reported in his *War Memoirs*:

> When our difficulties were solved through Dr. Weizmann's genius, I said to him: "You have rendered great service to the State, and I should like to ask the Prime Minister to recommend you to His Majesty for some honor." He said: "There is nothing I want for myself." "But is there nothing we can do as a recognition of your valuable assistance to the country?" I asked. He replied: "Yes, I would like you to do something for my people." . . . That was the fount and origin of the famous declaration about the national Home for Jews in Palestine. . . . Dr. Weizmann with his discovery not only helped us to win the War, but made a permanent mark upon the map of the world.

Although the prime minister's description of events makes Weizmann's task in securing the Balfour Declaration sound easy, the actual process was not at all simple. As World War I progressed, Britain found itself in an increasingly contradictory position in the Middle East. At the same time that leading members of the government were listening to Zionist aspirations, these same ministers were trying to stay on good terms with the Arabs. Arab nationalism intensified during this period, and Great Britain wanted Arab loyalty — and Arab oil. For this reason, many British officials did not want to risk antagonizing the Arabs by an official show of support for a Jewish state in Palestine.

Britain was also negotiating with France in an attempt to carve out mutually agreeable spheres of influence in the Middle East. Toward that end, in May 1916 the two countries signed the Sykes-Picot Agreement, a secret pact stipulating that the two powers would rule the vast area bounded by the Mediterranean, the Red Sea, the Arabian Sea, and the Persian Gulf. Specifically, the framers of the agreement envisioned a Holy Land parceled out into British, French, and Arab spheres of influence; the Jews were hardly mentioned in the pact.

When Weizmann and his fellow Zionists finally got wind of these developments, they were outraged. Weizmann blasted the agreement, protesting, "This is dividing the skin of the bear before it is killed!" He was worried on several counts: about the fate of the Jewish colonies in the Galilee, which was to be French territory; and, more important, about the overall fate of the Jewish state. He used all his powers of persuasion on his contacts in the British bureaucracy in an attempt to get Britain to back away from the terms of the Sykes-Picot Agreement.

Weizmann succeeded, and then some. His diplomatic tour de force, which resulted in the Balfour Declaration, prompted Charles Webster, a respected historian who was a junior official in the war office at the time, to marvel at Weizmann's uncanny diplomatic powers. "With unerring skill," Webster wrote, "he adapted his arguments to the special circumstances of each statesman. To the British and Americans he could use biblical language and awake a deep emotional undertone; to other nationalities he more often talked in terms of interest."

With the issuance of the Balfour Declaration, Weizmann had become, in the eyes of many Jews, a "Great Emancipator" as important to their cause as Abraham Lincoln had been to the American antislavery movement. For these Jews, the Balfour Declaration was the embodiment of all their long-cherished hopes. But the vaguely worded document was flawed: It alluded to, but did nothing to solve, the problems of fairly partitioning land between Palestine's Jewish and non-Jewish populations. The battle for a Jewish state in the Holy Land was far from over. As Vera Weizmann remarked of the Balfour Declaration, "Like most diplomatic documents, it tried to please too many people — and succeeded in pleasing too few! Yet it represented the beginning of the great adventure which brought the Jewish people home after almost two thousand years."

> [Lloyd George's comment] makes it appear that the Balfour Declaration was a reward given me by the Government. . . . I almost wish that it had been as simple as that, and that I had never known the heartbreaks, the drudgery and the uncertainties which preceded the Declaration.
> —CHAIM WEIZMANN

5

Gains and Setbacks

On March 8, 1918, Weizmann departed for the Holy Land as the head of a Zionist commission established by the British government to review the situation in Palestine and offer advice on settlement and development there. Stopping first in Alexandria, Egypt, and then journeying via the coastal road to the Holy Land, Weizmann arrived — to a hearty welcome — in a country on the brink of historic events.

It appeared as if the long-sought dissolution of Ottoman rule was at hand. On December 9, 1917, England's formidable general Edmund Allenby had conquered Jerusalem. By the time of Weizmann's arrival, Allenby's armies held a line north of Tel Aviv and were poised for a final assault on the Turks.

The political forces marshaled by Weizmann also appeared to be formidable. Indeed, just four days before leaving for Palestine, he met with England's king George V, who expressed his good wishes for the Zionists' success. But once Weizmann arrived in the Holy Land, he was forced to confront a number of disturbing realities.

Palestine is surprisingly beautiful now, but something sad and grave hangs in the air and all that is so senseless . . . this war among the lemon and orange groves.
—CHAIM WEIZMANN
in a 1918 letter to Vera

On December 9, 1917 — one month after the Balfour Declaration was issued — Jerusalem fell to British forces led by General Edmund Allenby, ending 400 years of Ottoman Turkish rule over the Holy City. In this photo, the city's mayor stands beneath a flag of surrender while two British sergeants look on.

Weizmann arrives in Tel Aviv, Palestine, in 1918. As British forces secured their hold on Palestine in the last months of World War I, Weizmann toured the country as head of a British commission looking into the large-scale establishment of Zionist settlements there.

First, World War I was still raging. In fact, Turkey's allies, the Germans, were launching a major offensive in Europe. Weizmann found that British politicians were more interested in following the battles there than with implementing the Balfour Declaration in Palestine. Second, Arab nationalism was becoming a potent force in international politics. The Arabs had helped the British during the war and felt that they were due something in return. Often, they were quite passionate about their demands — and quite resentful of the growing Jewish community in Palestine. Anti-Zionist propaganda stressed that it was time for the Arab nation "to awaken from its torpor, and to rise up in defense of its land, of its liberty, of its sacred places against those who were coming to rob it of everything."

Weizmann knew it was important that he establish some contact with the Arabs and thus arranged to meet with Emir Faisal, the commander in chief of the Arab army, to see if the two could find any common ground. The night before the parley, Weizmann journeyed to a desert site north of the city of

Aqaba. There, with British soldiers ringing the camp, Weizmann went for a walk, planning what he would say to Faisal and simply taking in the scenery. As he wrote in *Trial and Error*:

> It was a brilliant moonlit night . . . [and] as I stood there I suddenly had the feeling that three thousand years had vanished, had become as nothing. Here I was, on the identical ground, on the identical errand, of my ancestors in the dawn of my people's history, when they came to negotiate with the ruler of the country for a right of way, that they might return to their home. . . . Dream or vision or hallucination, I was suddenly recalled from it to present-day realities by the gruff voice of a British sentry: "Sorry, sir, I'm afraid you're out of bounds."

At the meeting the next day, Weizmann discovered that Faisal was more interested in Syria than Palestine, at least for the time being. Thus, the two were able to work out a broad compromise. Their promises were later put into writing, but events subsequently overtook the shaky pact.

Weizmann (left) with the Arab nationalist Emir Faisal. Weizmann met with Arab leaders to seek their approval of Zionist resettlement plans. Eventually Britain and France granted Faisal the kingdom of Iraq; his brother Abdullah was given control of the lands east of the Jordan River.

Weizmann also had to grapple with the differences between his views and those of the Jewish leaders in Palestine. Leading figures in the Yishuv, such as David Ben-Gurion, a Polish Jew who had come to Palestine in 1906, were more militant than Weizmann. They were dissatisfied with the ambiguous words of the Balfour Declaration and pointedly asked Weizmann why he had not asked outright for a Jewish state.

Even his visit to Jerusalem, the capital of the ancient Hebrew empire, was far from an enchanted homecoming. Fifty years earlier, Mark Twain, the celebrated American author and humorist, had journeyed to the ancient capital and grieved over "the stateliest name in history losing all its grandeur to become a pauper village." Weizmann found that not much had changed: Buildings were crumbling, and a large part of the population remained destitute.

To his chagrin, Weizmann found that the Balfour Declaration was not very well known in the Holy Land. In fact, the document was not officially published in Palestine until 1920. He decided that some symbolic act was needed to show the world that the declaration, and Zionism in general, were historical realities to be reckoned with, not empty promises and wild-eyed dreams.

A 1918 photograph of Weizmann (left), Allenby, and the two chief rabbis of Palestine. Britain ruled the territory after the war under a League of Nations mandate. When the Balfour Declaration became law, large-scale Jewish immigration quotas were set and a Jewish Agency established.

David Ben-Gurion, a Polish Jew who first came to Palestine in 1906. Ben-Gurion, a more militant Zionist than the moderate Weizmann, vied with Weizmann for leadership of the movement for years, eventually prevailing when he became Israel's first prime minister in 1948.

On July 24, 1918, Weizmann gathered the local notables, both Arab and Jew, and dedicated the cornerstone of the Hebrew University. His longtime dream was finally becoming a reality. Weizmann addressed the assembled crowd with a message of hope: "Intended primarily for Jews, [the university] will of course give an affectionate welcome to the members of every race and creed. For my house will be called a house of prayer for all the nations. Here the wandering soul of Israel shall reach its haven."

Weizmann was further heartened when Palestine fell to the British two months later. The Germans and Turks capitulated in October, and Weizmann headed home to England. His next task was to represent Zionist claims at the Versailles peace conference, to be held outside Paris in 1919. The Versailles meeting and another parley held at the Italian seaport of San Remo marked the first real opportunities for Zionist representatives to make their case before an assembled force of world leaders — leaders with the power to act on what they heard.

Weizmann stuck to his favored negotiating tactic of asking not for the "world" but for goals that were practical yet still worthy of the imagination. Once these goals were achieved, he planned to move on to the next set of demands. Some Zionists — notably Ben-Gurion and others in the Yishuv — disapproved of Weizmann's methods. They were more impatient and less interested in mollifying the great powers. But Weizmann was too powerful within the movement to be swayed by their arguments.

Weizmann, seated at center, with a group of Arab sheiks. Despite his negotiations with Arab leaders and with the more militant Zionists, Arab-Jewish violence broke out in Palestine in 1921; the British responded by sharply limiting Jewish immigration.

Now was the time, he felt, to ask not for the state itself but for conditions — such as increased immigration — that would lead inevitably to the creation of a Jewish state in Palestine. Speaking before the statesmen who had assembled to decide the fate of much of the postwar world, he sketched out his aspirations for the Holy Land. He told them of his hope that Jewish settlers would "gradually develop in Palestine a Jewish life as Hebraic as life in England is English. Only when this nationality forms the majority of the population shall the movement come to claim the government of this country."

Again running into the wall of international politics, Weizmann's calls were somewhat overshadowed (as were similar entreaties made by the Arabs) by other business. But the San Remo agreement did award Great Britain an official mandate to administer Palestine and did incorporate the Balfour Declaration into the terms of that mandate. This was no small achievement, for it meant that the Balfour Declaration had become a part of international law. The terms worked out in San Remo also allowed large numbers of Jews to immigrate to Palestine and stipulated that Hebrew, English, and Arabic would be the region's official languages. Given this good start, Weizmann would devote most of the 1920s to his Zionist activities, leaving science aside.

He was troubled to find that an erstwhile ally, British official Herbert Samuel, was not the champion of the Jewish people that Weizmann believed him to be. Samuel had been appointed high commissioner for Palestine in 1920, a move that had pleased Weizmann greatly, because Samuel was known as a committed Zionist. But in the wake of Arab-Jewish violence in the city of Jaffa in 1921, he ordered the temporary suspension of Jewish migration to the region. That same year, he allowed Haj Amin el Husseini, an Arab nationalist and an inveterate anti-Zionist, to take his hereditary post as grand mufti of Jerusalem. This was a religious office carrying great political and spiritual responsibility. In this way, Samuel had hoped to convert a "troublemaker" — Husseini had been imprisoned for his role in anti-Jewish disturbances — to his side. But Samuel's gambit was not successful, and Husseini would foment several bloody anti-Semitic uprisings in Palestine during the coming years.

Weizmann soon discovered that Samuel's positions reflected a trend in British policy: The government's commitment to Zionism had begun to waver. In 1921, Winston Churchill, then Britain's colonial secretary, journeyed to Palestine. There he established Abdullah (Faisal's elder brother), a Bedouin chieftain from Saudi Arabia, as the administrator of all the lands east of the Jordan River, a region then known as Transjordan. Transjordan, like Palestine, was governed under a British mandate. Fearing that Abdullah would create an international incident by marching on French-controlled Syria to claim the throne there, Churchill decided to give Abdullah a land to govern. Faisal, meanwhile, was awarded the kingdom of Iraq. Frustrated by these British concessions to Arab nationalism, Weizmann turned his attention to the United States, hoping to further enlist the aid of American Jewry and the U.S. government in building a Jewish nation.

His attempts, however, were hampered by his uneasy relationship with many American Jewish leaders, notably Supreme Court Justice Louis Brandeis.

British prime minister Lloyd George with his aides in Italy at the postwar San Remo Conference, at which Britain was awarded the mandate over Palestine. Weizmann's work in chemistry, crucial to the British victory, had earned him the high esteem of Lloyd George and the British government.

The Allenby Bridge across the Jordan River, connecting Palestine and the desert lands of the Transjordan. Arab nationalists wanted Palestine as an Arab state, but the British relegated them to the east in Transjordan, later known as the Kingdom of Jordan.

America's leading Zionist, Brandeis had supported Weizmann's efforts to secure the Balfour Declaration, but the two leaders had very different backgrounds. Brandeis was a prominent American and had come to the cause late in life; Weizmann was an uprooted child of the Pale. The two men also had very different views of the future of Zionism. After one run-in with the justice, Weizmann was so upset that he penned some biting remarks about him: "Brandeis is an American first and a Zionist only a few minutes in the day, and therefore has lost touch with Jewry and with the actualities of Palestine." Weizmann biographer Norman Rose has speculated that Weizmann disliked Brandeis largely because "Brandeis was the one serious competitor to Weizmann's leadership."

On April 2, 1921, Weizmann arrived in New York City for the first of many important trips to America. Several Jewish dignitaries, including Nobel Prize-winning physicist Albert Einstein, greeted his arrival, as did thousands of supporters, who had come to get their first look at the already legendary figure. Fanning out across the country, Weizmann and his supporters sought to bypass Brandeis and drum up American enthusiasm for Weizmann's brand of Zionism. They were quite successful, and Weizmann, haunted by the pitiful financial state of the movement, managed to turn America into Zionism's great "provider" during the 1920s.

He was able to do this by circumventing his critics within the American Zionist leadership and appealing directly to the people. Biographer Barnet Litvinoff described his tactics this way: "Weizmann cast a charm over America, confirming his supremacy in the Jewish world for years to come. . . . He troubled them little with ideology, but proffered the expectation of a new Jewish world arising in the ancient east as this one had arisen in the modern West. He refused to humble himself, or make Zionism into a charity."

Weizmann made a number of trips to the United States during the next several years, garnering support and much-needed funds for the Zionist cause. But his biggest triumph of the period was the creation of the Jewish Agency for Palestine in 1929, a broad-based, international organization that would work alongside other Zionist groups to promote the establishment of a Jewish homeland. Weizmann served as the organization's president.

He had to maintain a dizzying schedule in order to keep up with his many speaking, planning, and negotiating commitments. In 1927 he wrote his wife that he was "weary of the constant round of speeches, fund-raising, and so on." But his hard work paid off: As the 1920s drew to a close, his primacy in world Jewry was unquestioned. He was the founder and leader of the Jewish Agency for Palestine, had been president of the World Zionist Organization since 1920, had served as a primary force behind Hebrew University, and had secured the groundbreaking Balfour Declaration.

But the volatile political climate in Europe and Palestine made it impossible for Weizmann to rest on his laurels. In 1929 a summer-long Arab uprising sparked by Grand Mufti Husseini took the lives of more than 100 Jews and destroyed untold amounts of property. According to Litvinoff, "The land had not known a disaster of such magnitude, neither in the period of Turkish control nor during the war years. The Jews could think of a parallel only in the Russia of the 17th century." Palestine, the region that Jews had hoped would be a haven for them, had become a battleground.

Weizmann in New York City in the 1920s. Weizmann's efforts to raise funds for Jewish Palestine were especially successful in New York, where many German Jews had arrived in the mid-19th century and where many Eastern European Jews had arrived around 1900.

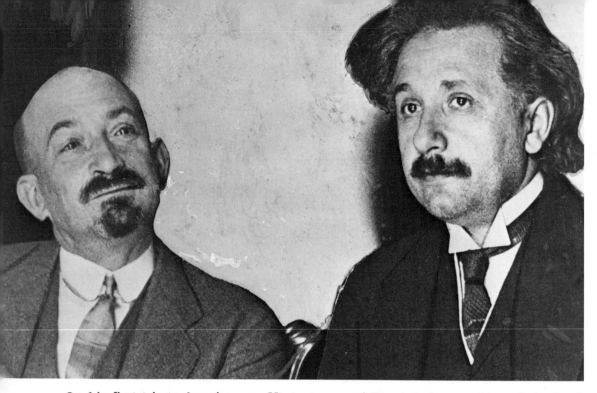

On his first trip to America on behalf of the Zionist movement in 1921, Weizmann met the great German Jewish physicist Albert Einstein and many other leading Jewish figures. Although his trip was successful, Weizmann clashed with Supreme Court justice Louis Brandeis over the scope of Zionism.

Historians and Zionists have criticized the leaders of the movement to secure a Jewish homeland for their relative lack of an "Arab policy." Unlike many of his associates, Weizmann was guilty of this only in his earliest years as a Zionist. By 1929 he was certainly a fierce believer in justice for the Arabs. Speaking before the Zionist congress gathered that year in Zurich, Weizmann said that the Jews must cultivate "genuine friendship and cooperation with the Arabs to open the Near East for Jewish initiative. Palestine must be built without violating the legitimate interests of the Arabs. Not a hair on their heads shall be touched." He went on to say that the 600,000 Arabs living there "have exactly the same right to their homes in Palestine as we have to our National Home."

The 1930s brought new challenges to Zionist leaders, and to Chaim Weizmann in particular. In reaction to the violence of 1929 the British severely restricted Jewish immigration and limited Jews' land purchases — the very foundations of Zionist activity in Palestine. Anti-British demonstrations quickly broke out in London, Poland, the United States, South Africa, and Palestine, and it appeared that Anglo-Zionist relations had been shattered.

Weizmann, furious at Britain's lukewarm support of the Jews in Palestine and saddened by the general tenor of events, resigned as president of the World Zionist Organization and the Jewish Agency for Palestine in 1930.

At the Zionist congress held the following year in Basle, Switzerland, Weizmann found himself under fire. Jabotinsky, in particular, took an extremely vocal, tough stand against Weizmann's record. The zealous leader called Weizmann's measured approach inadequate, and demanded that a Jewish state be set up on both sides of the Jordan River. This plan was highly impractical because the Transjordan, the region governed by Emir Abdullah, was almost entirely Arab. Undaunted by the logistics — and the inevitability of violence if large numbers of Jews moved into the area — Jabotinsky and his followers wanted to establish a Jewish majority in both Palestine and the Transjordan. Angered by what he considered to be an irresponsible and dangerous proposal, Weizmann met with a reporter and uttered words that sounded to the congress like her-

Chancellor Adolf Hitler addresses the German Reichstag in Berlin. Hitler, the leader of the Nazi party, rose to power in the national elections of 1933 on a platform of militarism and anti-Semitism; systematic discrimination and government-sponsored violence against Jews soon followed.

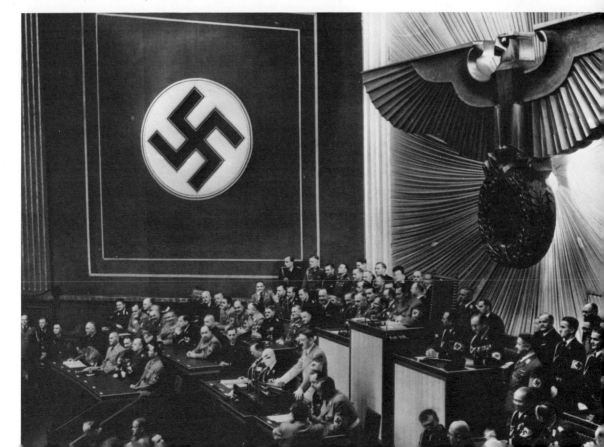

Weizmann in his laboratory in Rehovot, Palestine, where he was director of the Daniel Sieff Research Institute. In 1935 he was named the head of the Jewish Agency and president of the World Zionist Organization, posts he had previously held in the late 1920s and early 1930s.

esy: "I have no understanding of, and no sympathy for, the demand for a Jewish majority in Palestine. Majority does not guarantee security, majority is not necessary for the development of Jewish civilization and culture. The world will construe this demand only in the sense that we wish to acquire a majority in order to drive out the Arabs."

The statement caused an uproar. In an unprecedented motion, Weizmann was censured. When American Jewish leader Rabbi Stephen Wise lashed out against him, saying, "You have sat too long at English feasts," Weizmann stormed out of the meeting hall. Not surprisingly, he was not asked to resume the presidency of the World Zionist Organization. He was replaced — though not by Jabotinsky, who had sought the post, but by Nahum Sokolow, a Polish writer and longtime Zionist luminary.

Dissension within Jewish ranks could not have occurred at a worse moment, for in Germany Adolf Hitler was rapidly consolidating his power as head of the Nazi (National Socialist) party. Hitler became Germany's ruler in 1933 by portraying himself as a powerful leader devoted to the German "fatherland." His grandiose images appealed to many Germans as an antidote to crushing economic difficulties and the humiliation of their country's devastating loss in World War I. Hitler also advanced racist policies, declaring that Germany's Aryan population (non-Jewish Caucasians, especially those of Nordic ancestry) was a "pure" race destined to rule the world. The Jews, he claimed, had "soiled" Germany and were responsible for all of society's ills. Thus, the Jews of Germany faced constant harassment and humiliation. They were discriminated against in terms of jobs, housing, and education. With ominous frequency, Jews were beaten, ridiculed, and forced to live in ghettos. Such appalling practices became official in 1935 with the passage of the Nuremberg Laws, which legalized discrimination against Jews.

Weizmann followed these events from the vantage point of his second home in Rehovot, Palestine, a small village about 14 miles south of Tel Aviv. There he spent time with his wife and sons and began to pursue personal projects, notably the Daniel Sieff Research Institute. Daniel Sieff, a friend of the Weizmanns' son Michael, had taken his own life. When Daniel's parents told Weizmann that they wanted to set up a memorial for their son, he advised them to establish an agricultural research facility in the boy's name. Daniel's father, Israel, was the director of a successful chain of British stores, and his funds made the project a reality in 1934.

Meanwhile, England, despite the rise of anti-Semitic oppression in Hitler's Germany, continued to limit Jewish immigration, refusing to allow Palestine to become a haven for German refugees. The Zionists found to their chagrin that with Weizmann on the sidelines their movement lacked a figure with sufficient stature to deal with this affront. Though David Ben-Gurion had become the leading figure in the Yishuv, it was generally felt that he was not as effective on the international stage. Sokolow, too, though competent and conscientious, lacked Weizmann's fire and savvy.

Given the urgency of the circumstances, Weizmann found that he could not remain an exile from Zionist politics for long. Thus, at the 1935 Zionist congress, he was reinstated as president. Because the leadership of the World Zionist Organization was tied to the presidency of the Jewish Agency for Palestine, he also assumed that post. David Ben-Gurion was named to the newly created position of chairman of the agency. Some of the other leading Zionists vowed to keep a close watch on Weizmann's actions, but he ignored the uneasy atmosphere and applied himself to the task at hand. He announced that "the only dignified and really effective reply to all that is being inflicted upon the Jews. . . . is the edifice erected by our great and beautiful work in the Land of Israel. This alone is the real, proper, comforting and redeeming response to this tragedy. . . . Something is being created that will transform the woe we all suffer into songs and legends for our grandchildren." But for the Jews of Europe and Palestine, things would get far worse before they got better.

6

The Wages of War

Despite British-imposed quotas, the rise of Hitler led to a sharp increase in both legal and illegal immigration to Palestine; by 1939 some 450,000 Jews had entered the country. At the same time, the local Arabs were calling for the creation of an Arab state in the region. They had seen neighboring Arab states — Syria, Transjordan, and Iraq — move toward independence and autonomy and wanted the same for themselves. As Jewish and Arab nationalists continued to compete over the same tiny sliver of land, Palestine was becoming a tinderbox.

On April 19, 1936, an uprising commonly known as the Arab Revolt erupted. Mobs of Arabs rioted through the port city of Jaffa, murdering 16 Jews. A few days later, Arab leaders formed a supreme committee and organized a general strike, vowing to shut down shops and factories until Great Britain stopped all Jewish immigration and created an independent Arab state in Palestine. When the British ignored their demands, the rebels mined roads, derailed trains, and committed other acts of sabotage.

The world is gradually, relentlessly and effectively being closed to the Jews, and every day I feel more and more that a ring of steel is being forged around us.
—CHAIM WEIZMANN
on the rise of Hitler

A streetcar restricted to Jews in the Warsaw Ghetto during World War II. Many Jews fled Europe before the start of the war, but most remained behind. The Nazis and their allies systematically killed 6 million Jews during the war, most of them in death camps built throughout Germany and Poland.

At Munich in 1938, British prime minister Neville Chamberlain (left) and French premier Edouard Daladier (second from left) granted part of Czechoslovakia to Hitler in exchange for a pledge of nonaggression, which Hitler broke in 1939 when he invaded Poland. To Hitler's left stands Italy's dictator Benito Mussolini.

When Chaim and Vera Weizmann arrived back in the Holy Land after a sojourn in England, they felt as if they had entered an armed camp. Wherever Weizmann traveled, he was protected by sharpshooters of the Haganah, the unofficial Jewish defense force. Appalled by the violence and frustrated by the indecisiveness of the British authorities, Weizmann was determined to take matters into his own hands. Although he knew that his actions would outrage many in the Yishuv, he sent an emissary to Grand Mufti Haj Amin el Husseini, informing him that he would put a temporary halt to Jewish immigration if that would put an end to the smoke and guns. But Weizmann's intermediary brought back a disturbing telegram: "Haj Amin deems it a shame on the Arabs and on himself to accept any compromise coming from a Jew. Who is this Weizmann who will offer us a compromise and we to accept it? No, we refuse it. We need stoppage of immigration, and from the government."

In the face of ongoing violence, Britain brought in 20,000 extra troops to restore order. In addition, in 1937 the government appointed a commission, to be headed by Lord William Robert Wellesley Peel, to investigate the situation and make recommendations. Appearing before the commission, Weizmann delivered a powerful oration on the Jewish predicament: "There are in [central and eastern Europe] 6,000,000 people doomed to be pent up in places where they are not wanted and for whom the world is divided into places where they cannot live and places which they cannot enter." He went on to warn that despair and violence would plague Jewish communities around the world "unless some hope is given to the young people that one day, in some distant future, one in five, one in ten, one in twenty, will find a refuge somewhere where he can work, where he can live, and where he can straighten himself up and look with open eyes at the world and at his fellow men and women." Weizmann's eloquent testimony greatly impressed his audience. Even David Ben-Gurion, who had been outraged by Weizmann's overture to Husseini, felt compelled to say: "I do not think there is in the whole of Zionist literature anything as profound, as awe-inspiring, as penetrating, or as true."

Nevertheless, Weizmann had little hope that the Peel Commission would benefit the Zionists. Britain, it seemed to him, had a history of appointing such commissions in times of crisis merely as a way of defusing tension. Whatever recommendations were made rarely addressed the core issues. He knew, too, that the Arabs had also put forth a strong case before the commission. And Weizmann was well aware that Britain was very concerned with the Arab community in Palestine. Arabs still greatly outnumbered Jews in the region, and Britain relied on the Arab world for oil imports.

Weizmann was taken aback when the commission proposed a novel, startling idea that no one — neither the commission nor Weizmann — had yet considered in any detail: Palestine would be divided into two independent states — one Jewish, one Arab. The Arabs would control three-quarters of the territory in Palestine, and the Jewish state would occupy the remaining area. Cities such as Jerusalem, which held religious significance to both groups, would remain under British mandate. Thus was born the controversial concept of partition.

The area offered [the Jews] was so restricted as to make impossible the emergence of a viable Jewish state.
—MAURICE EDELMAN
British historian,
on the Peel Commission's
plan of partition

As he considered the plan, Weizmann found himself torn between opposing viewpoints. He was pleased that Britain appeared to be thinking in terms of an actual state for the Jews; this was a step beyond the Balfour Declaration's vague notion of establishing a Jewish "homeland." In addition, as a seasoned diplomat, Weizmann did not want to antagonize the British authorities by rejecting the proposal outright.

But support for the partition plan would draw criticism from Weizmann's fellow Zionists, many of whom found it difficult to swallow this reduced notion of Jewish statehood. At the 1937 Zionist congress, Weizmann and his political rival Ben-Gurion joined forces to appeal to the delegates for a mandate to continue negotiations on the plan. Both men felt that diplomatic efforts could eventually secure a larger Jewish state, but that a rejection of the plan might further imperil the Zionist dream. After days of impassioned oratory, Weizmann and Ben-Gurion managed to sway the congress.

An exhibition of anti-Semitic art in Berlin in 1938, indicative of the Nazis' stated effort to eradicate the Jews from Europe and make them an extinct people whose existence would be recorded only in anthropological museums.

But as they had in the past, the British authorities would soon disappoint Weizmann. On September 29, 1938, Prime Minister Arthur Neville Chamberlain joined the leaders of France and Italy in signing the Munich Pact with Adolf Hitler. The Germans had occupied Austria and parts of Czechoslovakia earlier that year, and the Munich Pact was an attempt to put a stop to German belligerence. The agreement stipulated that Germany would cease its hostility toward Czechoslovakia in exchange for control of the Sudetenland, a region of that country with a large German population. Given Hitler's insatiable appetite for territory and power, the pact would prove futile.

At the time, many Europeans were pleased with the agreement, which Chamberlain maintained would assure Europeans "peace in our time." But others denounced the pact and thought that France and England had demonstrated cowardice, not diplomacy. One English newspaper tersely remarked that "in Munich honor died." Weizmann shared this view and felt that England had betrayed the Czechs in a desperate attempt to keep up with the shifting demands of global politics. He feared that the Jews would meet the same fate.

As Weizmann had anticipated, Great Britain's international concerns began to affect its policy in the Middle East. The clouds of war were gathering, and Great Britain wanted to win the loyalty of Arab countries in order to protect the region's crucial naval bases and supply routes. Worried that the Arabs of the Middle East might side with Germany and Italy, the British government decided to abandon the idea of partition in order to court Arab support. Foreign Secretary Anthony Eden planned to have Saudi Arabian king Ibn Saud, a leading Arab nationalist, rule the entire region under British aegis. Rather than tell Weizmann outright of this change in policy, Eden again appointed a commission, this one chaired by Sir John Woodhead, to "look into" the concept of partition. Some Zionists sarcastically referred to this group as the "Re-Peel Commission." Its report, released in November 1938, stated that the partition of the Holy Land was "impracticable."

> For many years [Weizmann's] links with Britain were the secret of his great power. . . . But when Britain changed its policy and betrayed its promises, he was to pay with his position.
> —MICHAEL BAR-ZOHAR
> Israeli historian

A Jew being humiliated by Nazi militiamen in 1933, during the first wave of government-sponsored anti-Semitism in Germany. The rise of Nazism caused many Jews to emigrate to Palestine; by 1939, 450,000 Jews had arrived in the country.

That same month, as Weizmann and his fellow Zionists reeled from this blow, German Jews suffered through something worse as Hitler's storm troopers went on a rampage, beating and arresting Jews and destroying synagogues and Jewish-owned homes and shops. Known as *Kristallnacht* (Crystal Night) because of the shattered glass that littered city streets by morning, it marked the beginning of Hitler's "final solution" to the "Jewish problem." As the Jews of Europe would soon come to know, Hitler's "solution" was genocide — the deliberate extermination of a race.

As war appeared more and more certain, the British continued to fear that the Arabs might align themselves with Germany to achieve their aims in Palestine, just as they had fought with the British during World War I to throw off Ottoman rule. In an attempt to stave off this possibility, in May 1939, Britain issued a "White Paper" designed to placate the Arabs by renouncing the Balfour Declaration. Besides withdrawing their support for a Jewish state in the region, the government decreed that Jewish immigration would end following the admission of 75,000 immigrants during the next 5 years, thereby assuring an Arab majority in Palestine. The White Paper also called for a limitation on Jewish purchases of Arab land and proposed the establishment of an independent state with an Arab majority within 10 years. Jewish leaders were outraged; a livid Weizmann referred to the White Paper as a "death sentence" for Zionism.

As these objections were aired, World War II erupted. On September 1, 1939, German troops invaded Poland. Two days later Poland's allies France and Great Britain declared war on Germany. The stage was set for violence and upheaval that would effect people from Europe to the Orient.

Along with other groups that Hitler deemed "undesirable," Jews who had the misfortune to live under German rule were singled out for systematic extermination. Millions of Jews were shipped to concentration camps. Most were killed outright; others were used as slaves and then murdered. By the war's end, 6 million Jews would die as a result of the insane butchery historians have termed the Holocaust.

Weizmann wrote to Meyer Weisgal, an American Zionist friend, about the sense of doom brought on by Hitler's "final solution" as the seemingly unstoppable Nazi troops made inroads across Europe: "The foundations of everything in which we believe, and for which we live and work, are rocking and unless the onslaught of the German hordes is stopped in time, we shall all go under. I am confident that it will be stopped in the end; but when and at what cost, and what havoc may have been wrought meanwhile, no one can say. It is such thoughts as these that govern one's life at present, and everything else seems to have receded into the background."

During this period, both the Jews and Arabs of Palestine observed a relative truce with the British, who were consumed with the war effort. Britain allied itself with the United States, France, and others against the Axis powers of Germany, Italy, and Japan. Cooperation with the British put the Zionists in a particularly difficult situation, however. On the one hand, the British were fighting against the Nazi menace, to the obvious benefit of Jews and non-Jews everywhere. Accordingly, more than 30,000 Palestinian Jews joined the Allied armies. On the other hand, Britain repeatedly refused to ease its immigration policies in Palestine, turning a cold shoulder to desperate European Jews for whom escape to Palestine was the last hope. This apparent

Vera and Chaim Weizmann in London in 1939 at the start of the war. "Unless the onslaught of the German hordes is stopped in time, we shall all go under," he wrote. "It is such thoughts as these that govern one's life at present, and everything else seems to have receded into the background."

indifference to the fate of the Jews, coupled with the British repudiation of the Balfour Declaration, further infuriated the Zionists. They reacted by deciding to bring Jews into Palestine illegally.

The British responded by refusing to allow ships carrying illegal Jewish immigrants to enter Palestine. In one instance, several ships carrying thousands of European refugees were turned away from the shores of the Holy Land by British authorities. Some of the refugees were placed in internment camps on the island of Cyprus, south of Turkey; others were sent back to where they came from, an act that amounted to a death sentence for many. One group of 198 Jews defiantly blew up their ship, the SS *Patria*, after they were refused permission to dock in Palestine. As Vera Weizmann noted in her memoirs, "These men, women, and children perished in a vain endeavour to stir the conscience of mankind to allow the helpless victims of Nazi terror to enter the Homeland." Another ship, the SS *Struma*, carrying more than 750 desperate refugees on a vessel normally suited for about 100, sank off the coast of Istanbul after months in immigration limbo. At a mass demonstration protesting the *Struma* catastrophe, an outraged Weizmann exclaimed, "What a mockery to read the high-sounding phrases mouthed by the leaders of democracy, when their regulations are sending people deliberately to their death!" He lobbied British officials on behalf of the "coffin ships" that often fell prey to storms as they sought safe harbors, but he had only limited success.

Weizmann appealed to Winston Churchill, a longtime ally who had become prime minister in 1940. Churchill told Weizmann that "there's nothing [U.S. president Franklin Delano Roosevelt] and I cannot do if we set our minds to it." But Weizmann was disappointed when he met Roosevelt for the first time and found the president noncommittal regarding the concerns of Jews. In fact, it is said by many to be one of the enduring black marks on Roosevelt's record that he was not more forthright in support of the Zionists or more sensitive to the Holocaust taking place in Europe.

The Weizmanns' sons, Benjamin (left) and Michael, who joined Britain's Royal Air Force as a fighter pilot and was killed in February 1942. Benjamin felt distant from his father, who acknowledged that his devotion to Zionism and chemistry kept him apart from his family far too often.

Weizmann made several trips to the United States during the war, in all spending some 21 months there. Just before leaving on one of these journeys in February 1942, the Weizmanns were stunned by the news that their son Michael, a captain in the British Royal Air Force, had been killed in action. In many respects, Michael Weizmann was like his father — clever, witty, and gregarious. His death came as a devastating blow, especially because the Weizmann's other son, Benjamin, had been taken out of action earlier because he was suffering from shell shock.

The Weizmanns' relationships with their children had always been problematic. Consumed with the Zionist cause, Chaim Weizmann had little time for his sons and was disappointed that neither of them became involved in Zionism. Benjamin Weizmann had always been something of a problem child, and in his adult years he struggled with a drinking problem. Chaim was not blind to his less-than-ideal relations with his sons; at one point he wrote wrenchingly of the pain he felt at the situation: "Perhaps I have neglected my own family for the sake of the larger [family] which I have been trying to serve

Weizmann with Rabbi Stephen Wise at a May 1942 conference in New York, where the Zionist Congress voted to demand the establishment of an independent Jewish state in Palestine. The resolution represented a victory for Ben-Gurion and the more militant Zionists over Weizmann's moderate stand.

so faithfully. Benji and Michael each in their way are witnesses of my defeat. . . .We speak different languages . . . we are strangers." This state of affairs was captured most poignantly by something Benjamin Weizmann said to his mother in 1937: "It is high time this family was taken in hand by somebody, otherwise the Jews may have a National Home but we shall have none at all."

The month his son died, Weizmann had an article published in the prestigious and influential American magazine *Foreign Affairs*. The piece, which called unequivocally for a Jewish state in Palestine, formed the basis for the Biltmore Program, which was adopted during a May 1942 gathering of world Jewish leaders at New York City's Biltmore Hotel. This meeting was attended by more than 600 delegates of every Zionist persuasion — "practicals," "politicals," pro- and anti-Weizmann. Still shaken by his son's death, Weizmann attended the historic meeting. Many of the representatives, led by Ben-Gurion, were furious at the British and ready to take a new, militant stand on Palestine. Weizmann, labeled weak and indecisive, was held responsible for the blows the Zionist movement had received in re-

It looks as if one's private life must not interfere with the execution of one's duty.
—CHAIM WEIZMANN
on his inability to spend
time with his family

Former Israeli prime minister Menachem Begin speaking in 1982. In the 1940s, Begin was a leader of the Irgun, the underground guerrilla group that attacked British military posts and Arab civilians and fighters in a violent campaign to gain independence for a Jewish Palestine.

cent years. "We can no longer rely on people with a chronicle of failures and defeats behind them," one delegate shouted at Weizmann.

The program that emerged from the conference was more extreme — and anti-British — than a diplomat such as Weizmann might have devised. In calling for an end to Britain's mandate, the reopening of Palestine to Jewish immigration, and the establishment of a democratic Jewish state in Palestine, the Biltmore Conference issued a strong challenge to Great Britain. For all his grievances against the British, Weizmann still felt that they were the Zionists' best hope and was angered by the conference's defiant tone.

As the Biltmore Program demonstrated, Weizmann's pro-British stance brought him into increasing conflict with the Yishuv in general and with Ben-Gurion in particular. Indeed, Ben-Gurion was talking up the Biltmore Program as his personal "victory" and calling for the immediate immigration of 2 million Jews. Weizmann downplayed the Biltmore Program as "just a resolution, like the one hundred and one resolutions usually passed at great meetings," and charged that Ben-Gurion was "hurtful to the best interests of the movement, undermining my authority, and wasting my time." Weizmann even went so far as to say that he thought Ben-Gurion suffered from "mental aberrations." Ben-Gurion, for his part, accused Weizmann of being a closed-minded dictator who valued the opinions of the British authorities more than those of his Zionist comrades. As biographer Norman Rose pointed out, the conflict between the two men reflected much more than differences over the Biltmore Program or any other specific policy. Rather, this was "the classic confrontation in politics: between a young, capable, abrasive leader, anxious to get on, and an older statesman blocking his path and reluctant to relinquish his own grip."

Prime Minister Winston Churchill of Britain was committed to the eventual establishment of a Jewish state. During World War II, however, both he and U.S. president Franklin D. Roosevelt refused to bomb the death camps and did little to help Jewish refugees who fled the Nazi genocide.

The funeral of Lord Moyne, the British minister for Middle Eastern affairs, in Cairo in November 1944. He was assassinated by two members of the radical wing of the Irgun. Though most Jewish leaders condemned the act, the killing caused the British to reconsider their commitment to an independent Jewish state.

In October 1942, German and Italian forces were defeated at the battle of El Alamein in Egypt by Allied troops under the command of British general Bernard Montgomery. It was a turning point in the war, marking the beginning of the end of German domination of North Africa and removing the immediate Axis threat to the Middle East. As Allied victory grew more certain during the following year, some Zionist leaders in Palestine felt that the need for restraint toward the British had diminished. Some Jews even took up arms against them.

The Jews in Palestine had three main fighting forces. The Haganah was the primary Jewish security force and was subject to the authority of the Jewish Agency. The Haganah followed a general policy of *havlagah*, or restraint, which meant that it was a defensive force to be used only if Jews or their property were attacked. This was in keeping with the policies of both Weizmann and Ben-Gurion, who, though they differed regarding the British, did not want to antagonize the Arabs or jeopardize innocent lives.

The Irgun Z'vai Leumi (National Military Organization) was a militant group that, unlike the Haganah, did not limit itself to defensive measures. Its approximately 2,000 members adopted an aggressive approach to the British and the Arabs. The Irgun advocated active opposition to British rule in Palestine, although it agreed, at least initially, to cease anti-British activities during the war. The Irgun's advocacy of armed power and displays of force were condemned by the Jewish Agency and most of the Yishuv. Many found fault not only with the Irgun's violent practices but with its emphasis on making war at the expense of building such necessary institutions as settlements, hospitals, and service agencies for the future Jewish state.

An offshoot of the Irgun, the Lohamei Herut Israel (Fighters for the Freedom of Israel) was the most militant of the significant Jewish fighting forces in Palestine. Known by the Hebrew acronym of Lehi and to English speakers as the Stern Gang (after Avraham Stern, the group's founder), the group took the Irgun's policies to an extreme, often dealing in scattershot terrorism and political assassination.

In early 1944 the Irgun's leader, Menachem Begin (who would become Israel's prime minister in 1977) declared "war" on the British. During the next several months Irgun fighters bombed immigration, tax, and police offices in several cities, seized arms from a British camp, and even stole money from fellow Jews in order to fund the group's campaigns. Both the Irgun and the British suffered casualties during this outbreak of hostilities. The British deported captured Irgun and Lehi fighters to East Africa, and placed a reward on Begin's head.

The Irgun also incurred the wrath of Weizmann, Ben-Gurion, and the rest of the Zionist establishment, and they were labeled "maniacs, bandits, and nihilists" who "stabbed Zionism in the back." So passionate was the Zionist infighting that, at times, it appeared as if civil war might erupt among the Jews of Palestine.

Weizmann, living in his home in England, was dismayed by these developments in the Yishuv—but was even more horrified by the wholesale slaughter

Our people are at war with this regime—war to the end. There will be no retreat. Freedom—or Death!
—proclamation of the Irgun Zvei Leumi, declaring rebellion against British occupation, 1943

of European Jews at the hands of Hitler's Nazis. In Weizmann's view, the world seemed to have closed its eyes and ears. Indeed, even as reports of the true nature of Hitler's hideous assault on the Jews of Europe came to light, they were often dismissed as Zionist propaganda. The British stuck to the terms of the 1939 White Paper. Not wanting to give the impression that any country's "unwanted nationals" could be foisted upon Palestine, they rejected a Weizmann plea to make good on a Romanian offer to transfer 70,000 Jews to Palestine. A prophetic speech he made at New York's Madison Square Garden during this period had no effect except possibly to prick the world's conscience:

> When the historian of the future assembles the bleak record of our days he will find two things unbelievable; first the crime itself, second the reaction of the world to that crime. . . . He will be puzzled by the apathy of the civilized world in the face of this immense, systematic carnage of human beings. . . . Above all, he will not be able to understand why the free nations, in arms against a resurgent, organized barbarism, required appeals to give sanctuary to the first and chief victim of that barbarism. Two million Jews have already been exterminated. The world can no longer plead that the ghastly facts are unknown or unconfirmed.

The Allied leaders were largely unmoved by the pleas of Weizmann and others on behalf of the victims of genocide. They rejected a Zionist plan to send the Germans war matériel (equipment used in warfare) in exchange for Jews. They also refused to bomb the gas chambers and crematoria of the infamous Auschwitz concentration camp. Unable to stop the massacre of millions of men, women, and children, Weizmann plunged into deep despair. He and his wife had taken to carrying cyanide capsules in order to carry out a grim pact. If they were ever captured by the Nazis, they agreed that they would commit suicide rather than submit to the debasement they would face in one of Hitler's death camps.

On November 4, 1944, Weizmann had a meeting

with Prime Minister Churchill. This cordial talk took place just a week before Weizmann was due to depart for Palestine — his first trip there in five years. Churchill sounded very positive about the chances for a postwar resolution favorable to the Jews. Weizmann was hopeful that despite the enmity that had characterized Zionist-English relations during the past few years, Britain had not abandoned the Zionist cause.

Two days later this tentative agreement was shattered by an act of terrorism. Lord Walter Edward Guinness Moyne, Britain's minister for Middle East affairs and a close friend of Churchill, was assassinated in Cairo by two young Lehi members. The killing stunned the Jews, the British, and the world at large. *Haaretz*, the influential Jewish newspaper in Palestine, wrote, "Since Zionism began, no more grievous blow has been struck at our cause."

Weizmann, speaking to a Zionist group shortly afterward, said, "You all know my personal tragedy in losing my son. You can imagine how great was the shock to me. But the shock when I heard of the murder of Lord Moyne was not less. When my son was killed it was my personal tragedy. . . . but here is the tragedy of the entire nation."

Appalled by the murder of his friend, Churchill delivered a speech before the British House of Commons. The prime minister told the assembled legislators: "A shameful crime has shocked the world and affected none more strongly than those like myself who, in the past, have been consistent friends of the Jews and constant architects of their future. If our dreams for Zionism are to end in the smoke of assassin's pistols, and one labors for its future to produce only a new set of gangsters worthy of Nazi Germany, many like myself would have to reconsider the position we have maintained so consistently and so long in the past."

Churchill's anger proved that Weizmann had not exaggerated the devastating effects that pro-Zionist terrorism could have on the future of a Jewish state in Palestine. Weizmann hoped he could repair the damage before it was too late.

It was as though two men were locked in a danse macabre while millions stood in line waiting to be consumed by the flames licking at their feet.
—BARNET LITVINOFF
describing Roosevelt's and Chamberlain's procrastination in establishing an effective immigration policy for Jewish refugees

7

Out of the Ashes a State Is Born

Weizmann was uncertain about how he would be received when he returned to an uneasy Holy Land on November 15,1944. The Haganah was helping the British hunt down and arrest the Irgunists and Sternists. An Allied victory in World War II appeared virtually certain, although what that meant for Palestine was not.

Upon his arrival, Weizmann found that he was popular with the people of the Yishuv, if not with all of their leaders. As he made his way to cities and Jewish agricultural communities throughout the Holy Land, he was greeted with banners, school choirs, and celebrations. But although he was publicly lauded as the undisputed leader of the world Zionist movement, dissension continued to brew.

A European diplomat accustomed to the slow pace of change in Britain's corridors of power, Weizmann was dangerously out of step with the Yishuv. In an interview he gave shortly after his return from Palestine, he told a *New York Times* reporter that "We Jews will need some transitional period after this

> *[Weizmann] has carried his burden with patience and dignity, with serene concentration. His armor never buckled under the responsibility.*
> —LOUIS LIPSKY
> American Zionist

Some of the 4,500 Jewish death camp survivors aboard the ship *Exodus* are taken into custody by British soldiers at Haifa, Palestine, in October 1947 after British authorities refused them entry into the country. Worldwide outrage at Britain spurred the creation of the state of Israel.

Although tens of thousands of Jews tried to make their way into Palestine in the aftermath of World War II, British authorities set a monthly immigration limit of just 1,500. Many Jews entered the country illegally and were placed in detention camps; here Weizmann talks to some of the illegal immigrants.

war," and estimated that it would take perhaps 5 or 10 years for the Jewish community in the Holy Land to evolve into a state. This was an eternity as far as the Yishuv was concerned. As he had done in the past, Weizmann revealed his distance from the Jews working the land in Palestine. And even many foreign observers — Jew and non-Jew alike — felt that the Jewish people could be forgiven at this point for not wanting to leave their fate in the hands of others.

The year 1945 was pivotal for both world politics and the Zionist movement. In April, Franklin Roosevelt died and was replaced as president by Harry S. Truman, who would later surprise the Jews with his support of Zionism. Adolph Hitler committed suicide that same month, and Germany surrendered unconditionally a few weeks later. In July, Winston Churchill's Conservative party lost the election, and Weizmann's old ally left office without granting any more concessions to the Jews of the Holy Land. Churchill was replaced by Labor party politicians who had promised to rescind the White Paper of 1939 and work for the creation of a Jewish state in Palestine. Indeed, when Labor won the Zionists rejoiced, considering the election a clear victory for their cause. World War II finally ended in August as Japan, devastated by two atomic bombs dropped by the United States, surrendered.

To the surprise of many observers, Britain's new Labor government, headed by Prime Minister Clement Attlee and Foreign Secretary Ernest Bevin, soon made a mockery of the central tenets of Zionism. First, the British proposed a monthly immigration quota of 1,500 at a time when thousands of Jews, particularly those from Poland and Germany, were living in temporary camps and labeled "Displaced Persons." An indignant Weizmann was virtually ignored when he demanded the official renunciation of the White Paper and insisted that 100,000 Jewish immigrants be allowed into Palestine immediately. Bevin went on to offend even further by making a series of statements that appeared to make light of the Jews' suffering, among them that the Jews should not try and "get to the head of queue" with their demands, as postwar Britain had a lot of difficult international problems to work out. Given the callousness of England's leaders, Weizmann's cooperative approach to the British authorities lost credibility within the Zionist community.

Ben-Gurion, in a fury, asserted that "the acts of the British government are a continuation of Hitler's policy of hostility." He then did the unthinkable — he turned to the Irgun and Lehi and asked them to join the Haganah in forming a united resistance movement. The three groups did not merge their forces, but agreed to act in close concert with one another. This coalition, called the Hebrew Resistance Movement, swung into action in the autumn of 1945 with attacks against railway installations and British police targets. The groups also raided British stores of arms, destroyed planes belonging to the Royal Air Force, and blew up the bridges connecting Palestine to its neighbors.

By mid-1946, Palestine had become an armed camp, complete with bunkers, sandbags, motorized patrols, and 100,000 British soldiers and policemen. Yet the Jewish resistance, made up of just

5,000 fighters, held the British in check — and then some. As J. Bowyer Bell wrote in *Terror Out of Zion*: "The mandate became a garrison state under internal siege, and the garrison [military installation], despite its size, equipment, and determination, proved ineffectual and self-defeating."

A pacifist, Weizmann vehemently opposed Ben-Gurion and the new resistance movement, but given the situation, he did favor such unorthodox measures as illegal Jewish immigration and the setting up of unauthorized settlements. Rather than debate with Weizmann on areas of contention, the Hebrew Resistance Movement simply chose to keep him in the dark about what has been described as the "seamy side of Jewish political activities." As biographer Norman Rose pointed out, this might have been "the first stage in ousting [Weizmann] from effective leadership of the Zionist movement."

Realizing that the reins of power were slipping from his grasp and falling into the hands of those he distrusted, Weizmann threatened to end his leadership of the Zionist movement. Drawing on the teachings of Ha'am and his own commitment to nonviolence, Weizmann wrote:

Arab leaders meeting in Jerusalem in 1946 to plan a protest strike against Jewish immigration into Palestine. At the end of World War II, as violence between Arabs and Jews mounted, Arab nationalists stepped up their demands for an independent Arab state in Palestine.

Our only force is moral force — as we showed during all the years of the 'troubles.' It is the duty of our leaders to point out to our young people — the only valuable asset we possess — that they must concentrate on constructive achievement, however difficult that may seem. A policy of destruction can rebound only on ourselves, and it is we who, in the end, will be destroyed.

Political violence is one and indivisible. It is a method; and it is both inconsistent and useless to condemn one single act unless the whole method is discarded. . . . The events of the last few days indicate either a complete loss of control over the forces of destruction, or a change of policy (of which I know nothing). . . .

I cannot continue to play the part of a respectable facade screening things which I abhor, but for which I must bear responsibility in the eyes of the world.

For the time being, Weizmann stayed on as head of the World Zionist Organization and president of the Jewish Agency, but events would soon outpace him. On Saturday, June 29, 1946, the British began their most forceful and effective response to pro-Zionist terrorism — an operation that came to be known as Black Sabbath. Nearly 3,000 Jews were detained, among them some of Weizmann's allies in the movement, and a curfew was imposed. British soldiers swooped down on Tel Aviv, searching block by block and house to house for arms and for resistance fighters in hiding. The Irgun responded with the most violent attack ever aimed at the British in Palestine.

The British "nerve center" in Palestine, the headquarters of their administration, was the King David Hotel in Jerusalem, a luxury establishment overlooking the Old City. On July 22, 1946, 350 kilograms of dynamite exploded in the hotel, demolishing much of the building and killing 91 people — including 28 Britons, 41 Arabs, and 17 Jews. The operation had not been designed to claim so many casualties but to serve as a symbolic attack on British prestige. The incident has been called a "tragedy of errors" and remains one of the most controversial incidents in Israel's history.

> *Like Moses, Chaim Weizmann led the children of Israel through the wilderness before they again reached the Promised Land . . . and like him, Chaim too was often tempted to break the tablets of the Law.*
> —VERA WEIZMANN comparing Chaim to Moses

Jewish settlers welcoming Weizmann to their newly built village. As early as 1929, Weizmann espoused the importance of "genuine friendship and cooperation with the Arabs." The 600,000 Arabs of Palestine, he said, "have exactly the same right to their homes in Palestine as we have to our National Home."

The botched bombing of the King David Hotel signified the end of the united resistance movement. The Haganah issued a public statement claiming that "the Hebrew Resistance Movement denounces the heavy toll of lives caused in the dissidents' operation at the King David Hotel." The Haganah also disassociated itself from the Irgun, reverting to its old view of Begin's organization as a renegade band of terrorists. But although the bombing was reviled both inside and outside of Palestine, some historians have pointed out that it did, however, at least partly achieve its desired objective: Britain began to wonder if its presence in Palestine was more trouble than it was worth.

The Zionist congress of December 1946 marked a turning point in the movement and in the life of Chaim Weizmann. As he addressed the assembled delegates, the 72-year-old Weizmann was heckled as a demagogue — a leader who appeals to feelings and prejudice rather than the intellect. Weizmann defended himself eloquently and went on to caution the men and women present against following a path of violence and hasty judgments: "I warn you against bogus palliatives, against short cuts, against false prophets, against facile generalizations, against distortion of historic facts."

His speech was greeted with cheers and applause, but in the end, the Zionist delegates demonstrated that while they might still believe in the man, they had lost confidence in his methods. By a narrow margin, they voted against his proposal that he meet with Bevin to try to negotiate changes in British policy. The Yishuv had finally decided that its foreign-born and pro-British leader had little left to offer. Realizing that he had lost the faith of his constituency, Weizmann resigned from the presidency of the World Zionist Congress. He bowed out by affirming that "Zion will be redeemed through righteousness and not by any other means." It appeared as if his public life was finished.

Weizmann recorded his feelings about that fateful congress in *Trial and Error*: "I became, therefore, as in the past, the scapegoat for the sins of the British Government; and knowing that their 'assault' on the British Government was ineffective, the 'activists,' or whatever they would call themselves, turned their shafts on me. . . . [They] had made up their minds that I was to go."

The following spring, Great Britain, faced with the continued noncooperation of both the Jews and the Arabs, pronounced the mandate "unworkable." Bevin sought help from the recently created United Nations (UN) in finding a political solution and announced Britain's intention to withdraw from Palestine on May 15, 1948. The English role in Palestine was coming to an end.

Weizmann appeared before the UN Special Committee on Palestine (UNSCOP) on July 8, 1947. Though he no longer had any official post in the Zionist movement, UNSCOP had sought him out as the most knowledgeable and articulate champion of Zionism and world Jewry. As he had done in the past, Weizmann called for the partition of Palestine and the creation of a Jewish state.

Weizmann was perhaps most eloquent when he spoke of the pro-Zionist violence that had recently plagued the Holy Land. He told the committee that British policies, the White Paper in particular, had "released certain phenomena in Jewish life which are un-Jewish, which are contrary to Jewish ethics,

> *He was a proud Jew, who aroused deep respect. . . . Weizmann knew how to address [listeners] as his equals—forcefully, authoritatively, and even sharply—though never appearing haughty or arrogant.*
> —MICHAEL BAR-ZOHAR
> Israeli historian

Jewish tradition. 'Thou shalt not kill' has been ingrained in us since Mount Sinai. It was inconceivable ten years ago that the Jews would break this commandment. Unfortunately they are breaking it today, and nobody deplores it more than the vast majority of the Jews."

Weizmann's appearance before the UN committee also marked the beginning of his ultimately successful effort to lobby support for the inclusion of the Negev Desert in the territory that the Jews would receive under a UN partition plan. The Negev had not been set aside for the Jews in any earlier partition plan. Though it was a vast, mostly barren wilderness, Weizmann knew that with proper irrigation, the Negev had a vast potential for settlement and farming. And as a political realist, he also saw the region as a defensive buffer against neighboring Arab countries.

The Zionists' cause was assisted by a tragedy known as the *Exodus* affair. The *Exodus* was a ship that had tried to make its way — the White Paper notwithstanding — to the Holy Land packed with some 4,500 European Holocaust survivors. After a struggle with the Haganah in which three Jews were killed, the British commandeered the vessel off the coast of Palestine and eventually forced the beleaguered would-be immigrants back to West Germany. This sorry spectacle was acted out before the world's press, radio, and newsreel cameras. Despite the violence and the lives lost, this incident furthered the Zionist dream by swaying public opinion against immigration restrictions in Palestine.

This propaganda victory was tempered by another violent episode that occurred shortly afterward. The Irgun, in retaliation for the British-sponsored hanging of three Jewish escapees from the Acre prison fortress, kidnapped and hanged two British soldiers. Anti-Semitic riots erupted in cities across Great Britain. Yishuv relations with Britain, already bad, had sunk to their lowest level.

The UN vote on the partition of Palestine was scheduled for November 26, 1947. In October, Weizmann left England for the United States to embark on what Norman Rose called "one of the most intricate and dramatic lobbying exercises in modern diplomatic history." Weizmann addressed the United Nations, which was then meeting in Lake Success, New York. He lobbied individual United Nations delegates, encouraging those who supported partition not to falter and trying to change the minds of those against the plan. He also traveled to Washington, D.C., where he met with President Harry Truman to convince him of the Negev's importance to Israel. Later that afternoon, Truman told the chief American delegate to the UN that the Negev must be part of the Jewish state.

According to Israeli journalist Amos Elon, "The basic premise underlying the [partition] decision was that two intense nationalisms had clashed over the issue of Palestine. Both possessed validity and yet were totally irreconcilable. Regardless of the historical origins of the conflict, the rights and wrongs of the promises and counter-promises, the basic fact was the presence in the country of 650,000 Jews and 1,220,000 Arabs."

Jewish settlement throughout Palestine accelerated after the war. These settlers head south from Jerusalem into the Negev Desert in 1947; within a few years, advanced irrigation methods transformed the Negev from a sparsely populated wasteland into a fertile farming region.

Weizmann appearing before a United Nations commission in 1947. Britain turned the Palestine question over to the UN after militant Zionists killed 91 people in the 1946 bombing of Jerusalem's King David Hotel.

Weizmann, Ben-Gurion, and the mainstream Zionists reluctantly supported the partition plan. They reasoned that even a partitioned homeland was preferable to continued uncertainty and violence. Said one Zionist spokesman, "This sacrifice would be the Jewish contribution to the solution of a painful problem and would bear witness to the Jewish people's spirit of international cooperation and its desire for peace."

But many Arabs objected to the partition plan, believing that the Holy Land was theirs and had been for many centuries. They resented having a UN settlement forced upon them. Some Arab leaders claimed that European politicians supported partition simply to assuage their guilt over the treatment of the Jews during World War II. Certain militants even urged a united Arab effort to exterminate the Jews in Palestine.

As the day of the fateful UN vote drew near, Weizmann realized that the Jews did not have the votes necessary to win approval of the partition plan. Jewish Agency representatives resorted to filibustering — the use of tactics such as reading from the telephone book in order to delay a vote. This strategy bought Weizmann three extra days, during which he was constantly on the phone, lobbying. Despite his increasingly severe eye trouble and generally frail health, the 73-year-old Weizmann was tireless in his efforts.

The vote finally took place on November 29. The proceedings were broadcast worldwide, and it took just 3 minutes to arrive at the final tally: 33 for partition, 13 against, 10 countries abstaining. Relieved and elated, Weizmann broke down and wept.

That evening, he attended a triumphant Zionist rally. As Weizmann entered the arena, according to his longtime friend Meyer Weisgal, "the cheering engulfed the building. He was lifted out of my protective grasp on to the shoulders of his people and carried into the hall." To the strains of "Hatikvah" ("The Hope"), the song that would become the national anthem of the state of Israel, Weizmann was hailed by the jubilant, victorious Jewish masses. But the Zionist leader refused to be swept away by the ecstasy of the moment. He delivered a brief, cautionary message to the jubilant crowd: "The world will judge the Jewish state by its actions towards the Arabs."

Indeed, when the British began to withdraw from the Holy Land, Arab-Jewish relations became the central issue. Both groups tried to take advantage of the vacuum of power in order to strengthen their positions. Jews and Arabs engaged in guerrilla warfare, fighting over small bits of territory, as British soldiers watched from the sidelines. Five weeks after the UN vote, 600 residents of Palestine had been killed in the skirmishes. A full-scale war seemed imminent — and indeed was threatened by the surrounding Arab states — as the date of British withdrawal from Palestine grew closer.

Weizmann sailed for London in December, planning to rest there for a month before returning to his home in Rehovot. But in January 1948 word reached him that U.S. president Harry Truman was now in favor of postponing partition and setting up a UN trusteeship over Palestine. The threat of war in the region, coupled with the possibility that U.S. support for partition might cost America its Middle East oil supply, had brought on Truman's change of heart. After American Zionist leaders tried unsuccessfully to convince Truman to back the partition plan, they appealed to Weizmann for help.

When an exhausted Weizmann arrived back in the United States, however, the president refused to see him. It took the intercession of an old friend of Truman, a Kansas City haberdasher named Eddie Jacobson, to win Weizmann an audience with the president. Jacobson, a Jew who had served in an

> *There were many moments, during the long years of these conflicts about inner and outer policy, that shook men to the core. Weizmann delivered some of his most momentous addresses during this period and experienced some of his most grievous disillusionments as well as a few of his most unforgettable triumphs.*
> —NAHUM GOLDMAN
> American Zionist

Weizmann celebrates the creation of the state of Israel. On November 29, 1947, the United Nations voted 33–13 to partition Palestine into two independent states, one Jewish and one Arab. Weizmann had spent months lobbying the UN delegates, then headquarted in suburban New York, and waited out the vote in the city.

artillery battery with Truman during World War I, had remained a good friend to the president over the years. He spoke so highly of Weizmann to Truman — calling him a hero like the president's hero, Andrew Jackson — that the president finally agreed to give Weizmann a hearing.

Weizmann informed Truman that the Jews of Palestine would declare the establishment of their state on May 15, no matter what the United Nations decided. He left believing that his discussion with the president had made a world of difference, but some of his colleagues were not as confident. As David Ben-Gurion and others began forming a provisional government for the still-unnamed Jewish state, Weizmann was sure that come May 15, Truman would recognize the new nation.

On May 14, 1948, the British high commissioner for Palestine departed, formally ending Britain's mandate. That night, Ben-Gurion, speaking for the executive committee of the Jewish Agency and the

provisional government, proclaimed the establishment of the state of Israel, effective the next day. As Weizmann had hoped, Truman extended U.S. recognition immediately.

On May 15, Israel's first day of statehood, Weizmann received a telegram from Ben-Gurion: "On the establishment of the Jewish State, we send our greetings to you, who have done more than any other living man towards its creation. Your stand and help have strengthened all of us. We look forward to the day when we shall see you at the head of the state established in peace."

At least temporarily, the animosities and bitterness that had consumed the Zionist movement during the previous decade dissolved in the sheer elation of the nation's founding. Weizmann, by now frail and a long way from Motol, had lived to fulfill an incredible dream: He had been named president of the provisional government of the Jewish state, Israel.

8

The Weizmann Legacy

The world's Jews did not have much time to savor Israel's independence. Jubilation quickly gave way to grim determination, for the birth of the infant state was greeted by the invading Arab armies of Egypt, Syria, Iraq, Transjordan, and Lebanon, plus contingents from Saudi Arabia, Sudan, and Yemen. According to Arab propaganda, these forces would not rest until they had managed to "drive the Jews into the sea."

The war raged on into June, and the fighting was not stilled until an armistice agreement was signed in early 1949. By then Israel had prevailed, capturing more land than had been allotted in the UN partition agreement. Nonetheless, many Israelis believed that the state needed to expand further in order to give it more buffer zones like the Negev.

The Negev had been retained, as had most of Galilee, an area in the north. Israeli troops had also won control of the modern half (New City) of Jerusalem. But Syria controlled the Golan Heights, a region overlooking the Hula Valley in Israel's north.

The air is crystal pure, so pure that you can look back over three thousand years of history.
—CHAIM WEIZMANN
describing Palestine

Weizmann was 73 years old and in failing health when his lifelong dream of a Jewish homeland was realized in 1948, yet he continued to play an active role as Israel's first president and as international spokesman, organizer, and ambassador for Zionism.

On February 18, 1949, Weizmann was sworn in after his formal election as president of Israel. The post was a largely ceremonial one; the more significant office of prime minister was held by Ben-Gurion, Weizmann's old rival, who relegated him to the background in governmental affairs.

This area became a base from which Syrian gunners terrorized Israeli settlements below. Judea and Samaria, the biblical names for lands on the West Bank of the Jordan River, remained in Jordanian hands, which meant that at one point the Jewish state was just nine miles wide. The Jordanians also held on to the Old City of Jerusalem, with a "no-man's-land" of barbed wire and land mines separating the antagonists.

Still, the Jews had a nation of their own. Peace would come, many Israelis hoped, as soon as their Arab neighbors got over the initial shock of defeat and learned to live with the Jews, who were in Palestine to stay. In order to prove that point, 6,000 Jews had died during the war of 1948–49. Unfortunately, they would not be the last.

Weizmann returned to Israel in September 1948. To his dismay, he found that his position as president of the new republic of Israel was largely symbolic. In effect, Weizmann had become a bystander;

Prime Minister Ben-Gurion held all the real authority. Weizmann was revered as an experienced elder statesman but was expected to be nothing but a figurehead. One writer described this as Weizmann's "hollow glory." Surely, to have come so far to end up with virtually no say in affairs of state was, in Weizmann's mind, some sort of cruel joke.

Ben-Gurion insisted on keeping him out of the new nation's decision-making elite. He did not invite Weizmann to any cabinet meetings, nor would he even pass on the minutes from those meetings. And, in perhaps his most hurtful slight of the aging, increasingly ill national hero, he did not invite Weizmann to sign Israel's newly drafted Declaration of Independence, even though several lesser officials were accorded this honor.

At times, Weizmann was able to joke about his painful situation. According to one well-known anecdote, Weizmann dropped his handkerchief during a state ceremony. After a companion retrieved it,

A Jerusalem woman waves the Israeli flag. The surrounding Arab nations, opposed to the partition of Palestine from the start, invaded Israel in May 1948 in an effort to establish a Palestinian Arab state. In the fighting that ensued, the Israelis conquered much of the land the UN had set aside for the Arabs.

Weizmann before a crowd of 150,000 in New York on the first anniversary of Israeli independence. Funds raised for Israel among American Jews were vital to the state's existence; for example, in New York in 1949, a one-night event at which Weizmann presided drew $18 million in donations.

Weizmann was very effusive in expressing his thanks. When the person who had retrieved the handkerchief said that there was no need for him to be so appreciative, for he had only picked up a handkerchief, Weizmann is said to have responded, "Oh, but you must realize the importance of this handkerchief to me. Nowadays, this is the only thing I am allowed to poke my nose into."

Although Ben-Gurion had tied his hands politically, Weizmann stayed busy as the 1940s drew to a close. In February 1949 he was officially elected president of Israel. The Herut party, the political successor to the militant Irgun, ran a candidate against him, to cries of "shame" from most of Israel's public. That same month, Weizmann published his memoirs, *Trial and Error*, an occasion that was greeted by popular acclaim both in Israel and abroad. In April he traveled to New York, where his presence at a fund-raising event earned the nascent state an astonishing $18 million in donations in just one evening.

In 1949, one of his lifelong ambitions bore fruit with the inauguration of the Weizmann Institute of Science in Rehovot. But in this undertaking, too, Weizmann's postindependence experiences were far from joyful. The troubles had to do with the institute's director, David Bergmann, who was very close to the Weizmanns and was even said to be something of a surrogate son to both Chaim and Vera. Bergmann, in Weizmann's eyes, had done two unforgivable things: used the institute for war-oriented research and served as Ben-Gurion's scientific adviser. This embittered Weizmann so profoundly that in mid-1951 he fired Bergmann.

By the early 1950s, Weizmann's health had worsened considerably. He had coped with eye trouble for much of his life, but by now he was nearly blind with glaucoma, a degenerative condition caused by increasing pressure in the eye. And though he was still mentally alert, in late 1951 he fell seriously ill and remained virtually bedridden for the next year.

President Weizmann with women soldiers during the 1948 Israeli-Arab war. From independence on, Israel was the strongest military power in the Middle East, but the huge cost of maintaining its army would hobble the country's economy and make it dependent on the United States for support.

On November 9, 1952, he lapsed into a coma, suffered two heart attacks, and died. He was just days short of his 78th birthday.

The fallen Zionist leader was mourned throughout the world. In Israel, his funeral was attended by so many people that it had to be extended for another day. Weizmann's burial, too, spoke of the dramatic life he had led — he was laid to rest in an open-sided coffin so that he would be in contact with the soil of the beloved land that had been his life's prime focus.

Speaking for all Israelis, Ben-Gurion eulogized the president: "Chaim Weizmann was a Prince of the Jewish Nation. . . . [He will] take his place in the eternal history of the Jewish people alongside the great figures of the past — the Patriarchs and Kings, Judges, Prophets and spiritual leaders who have woven the fabric of our national life for four thousand years."

Part of the Weizmann legacy to his new nation — and the world at large — is scientific. As a young man, his scientific genius enabled Great Britain to emerge from a munitions crisis that threatened to effect the outcome of World War I. And the Weizmann Institute of Science, built on the foundation of the Sieff Institute, has become a top-notch research facility for Israeli scientists as well as those from around the world.

But the most significant Weizmann legacy by far is that of his Zionism. Like the timeless words of Ahad Ha'am, his thinking remains vital today. In fact, many commentators have noted that Weizmann's death left a gap in the Israeli government. Without a man or woman of comparable vision, the country has been left with several capable and practical leaders, but few with a grand vision of what Israel should stand for in the eyes of its citizens or of the world at large. Few, in short, like Weizmann.

Israel has struggled into maturity, having weathered countless skirmishes and several wars with neighboring Arab states. The nation is still grappling with an issue Weizmann recognized as of the utmost importance: the relations between Jew and Arab. The ongoing nature of this problem is dem-

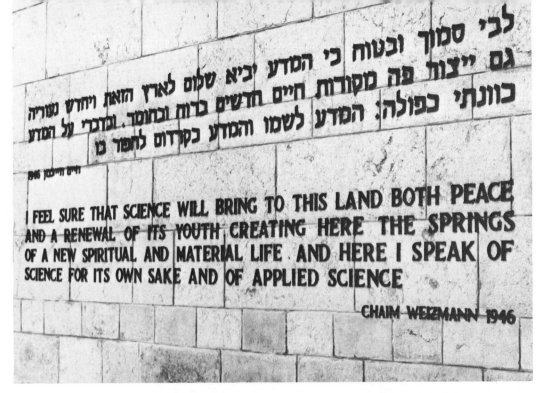

לבי סמוך ובטוח כי המדע יביא שלום לארץ הזאת ויחדש נעוריה ... ובדברי על המדע גם ייצור פה מקורות חיים חדשים ברוח ובחומר ... כוונתי כפולה: המדע לשמו והמדע כקרדום לחפור בו

חיים ויצמן 1946

I FEEL SURE THAT SCIENCE WILL BRING TO THIS LAND BOTH PEACE AND A RENEWAL OF ITS YOUTH CREATING HERE THE SPRINGS OF A NEW SPIRITUAL AND MATERIAL LIFE AND HERE I SPEAK OF SCIENCE FOR ITS OWN SAKE AND OF APPLIED SCIENCE

CHAIM WEIZMANN 1946

onstrated in news reports almost daily. A primary bone of contention between the two groups is the Israeli occupation of the West Bank, a region that has 1 million Arab inhabitants. Weizmann had ideas on leadership and Arab-Jewish problems as far back as his days with the Hovevei Zion in Russia's Pale of Settlement. Then and throughout his life he was convinced that Zionism could exist — and triumph — only as a moral force, as a force that kept justice at the fore, as a force that stood for the nonviolent resolution of disputes. Accordingly, given the tensions in today's Middle East, his name is now part of any important discussion on Israel's future. Weizmann, though politically eclipsed in his final days, has been revered by his compatriots and remembered by history.

More than any other individual, Weizmann — with his passion, intelligence, and vision — enabled the Jewish people to realize a nearly 2,000-year-old dream. As British diplomat Isaiah Berlin noted: "Chaim Weizmann was the first totally free Jew of the modern world, and the state of Israel was constructed, whether or not he knows it, in his image. No man has ever had a comparable monument built to him in his own lifetime."

Chaim Weizmann died on November 9, 1952, at the age of 77. His commitment to Zionism, peace, and scientific research is reflected in this monument in his adopted hometown of Rehovot, Israel, site of the world-renowned Weizmann Institute of Science.

Further Reading

Amdur, Richard. *Menachem Begin.* New York: Chelsea House, 1987.

Baker, Rachel. *Chaim Weizmann: Builder of a Nation.* New York: Julian Messner, 1958.

Berlin, Isaiah. *Chaim Weizmann.* New York: Herzl Institute, 1958.

Blumberg, Harold M. *Weizmann, His Life and Times.* New York: St. Martin's Press, 1975.

Elon, Amos. *Herzl.* New York: Holt, Rinehart & Winston, 1975.

———. *The Israelis: Founders and Sons.* New York: Holt, Rinehart & Winston, 1976.

Laqueur, Walter. *A History of Zionism.* New York: Holt, Rinehart & Winston, 1976.

Laqueur, Walter, and Barry Rubin, eds. *The Israel-Arab Reader.* New York: Penguin Books, 1975.

Litvinoff, Barnet, ed. *The Letters and Papers of Chaim Weizmann.* New Brunswick, NJ: Transaction Books, 1983.

———. *Weizmann: Last of the Patriarchs.* New York: Putnam, 1976.

Rose, Norman. *Chaim Weizmann: A Biography.* New York: Viking Press, 1986.

St. John, Robert, et al., eds. *Life World Library: Israel.* New York: Time Inc., 1965.

Shihor, Samuel. *Hollow Glory: The Last Days of Chaim Weizmann, First President of Israel.* New York: Thomas Yoseloff, 1960.

Vail, John J. *David Ben-Gurion.* New York: Chelsea House, 1987.

Weisgal, Meyer W., ed. *Chaim Weizmann: Statesman, Scientist, Builder of the Jewish Commonwealth.* New York: Dial Press, 1944.

Weizmann, Chaim. *Trial and Error.* New York: Harper & Brothers, 1949.

Weizmann, Vera. *The Impossible Takes Longer: The Memoirs of Vera Weizmann as told to David Tutaev.* New York: Harper & Row, 1967.

Zagoren, Ruby. *Chaim Weizmann: First President of Israel.* Champaign, IL: Garrard, 1972.

Chronology

Nov. 27, 1874	Chaim Weizmann born in Motol, Russia
1886	Studies in Pinsk
1892	Travels to Germany to further his education
1898	Attends his first Zionist congress in Basle, Switzerland
July 1904	Settles in England
1907	Visits Palestine for the first time
1914–18	World War I; Weizmann manufactures synthetic acetone for the British army
Nov. 2, 1917	Balfour Declaration issued
March 1918	Weizmann arrives in Palestine as head of Zionist commission
July 24, 1918	Dedicates cornerstone of Hebrew University
April 2, 1921	Arrives in New York to raise funds for Zionist cause
1929	Founds the Jewish Agency for Palestine and is elected its head
1930	Protests British White Paper by resigning the presidencies of the Jewish Agency and the World Zionist Organization
1935	Reinstated as president of the World Zionist Organization and the Jewish Agency
1936	Protesting Britain's pro-Zionist policies, Palestinian Arabs riot and take part in a general strike
May 1939	British White Paper renounces Balfour Declaration and restricts Jewish immigration to Palestine
1939–45	World War II
May 1942	Biltmore Congress meets
Nov. 29, 1947	UN votes for the partition of Palestine
May 15, 1948	British withdraw from Palestine; nation of Israel is proclaimed; Arab armies attack Israel
Feb. 1949	Weizmann elected president of Israel; his memoir, *Trial and Error* is published
Nov. 9, 1952	Dies in Rehovot, Israel

Index

Richard Amdur is a Brooklyn-based writer and editor. His articles have appeared in the *New York Times*, *Psychology Today*, and *Cosmopolitan*. He is the author of *40+ for Men: Your Guide to a Healthy Body and Mind*, published by Longmeadow Press, and *Menachem Begin* in the Chelsea House series WORLD LEADERS—PAST & PRESENT. For more than a year he lived on Kibbutz Tzorah in Israel.

Arthur M. Schlesinger, jr., taught history at Harvard for many years and is currently Albert Schweitzer Professor of the Humanities at City University of New York. He is the author of numerous highly praised works in American history and has twice been awarded the Pulitzer Prize. He served in the White House as special assistant to Presidents Kennedy and Johnson.

PICTURE CREDITS